On the cover:
Bauer (Stockholm, Sweden).
Designed by Dizel&Sate. Photo courtesy of Dizel&Sate.

Inside the front jacket flap:
Zaha Hadid and Suprematism (Zurich, Switzerland).
Designed by Zaha Hadid Architects. Photographed by Martin Ruetschi.

Inside the back jacket flap:
Leo Burnett Office (Singapore).
Designed by Ministry of Design. Photographed by CI&A Photography.

On page 001:
Reebok Flash (New York, USA).
Designed by Formavision. Photographed by Jordan Kleinman.

On page 005:
Ruby Lounge (Sydney, Australia).
Designed by Make Creative. Photographed by Nick Bowers.

On page 006:
SOQS (Nishinomiya, Japan).
Designed by KEIKO + MANABU. Photographed by Takumi Ota.

On page 009:
Wanderlust (Singapore).
Lobby wall feature designed by Asylum. Photograph courtesy of
Asylum.

On page 079:
ANNA (Basel, Switzerland).
Designed by ZMIK. Photographed by Eik Frenzel.

On page 125:
BOSS Orange (Special Concept Store) (Shanghai, China).
Graphics designed by Projekttriangle Design Studio. Interior designed
by RAISERLOPES architects//interior architects. Photographed by Tom
Ziora.

On page 201:
Ara Pizza (Sant Quirze del Vallès, Spain).
Designed by Pablo Téllez. Photographed by Juan Ventura.

On page 251:
NY 11-18-02-10 (New York, USA).
Designed by Campaign. Photographed by Frank Oudeman.

On page 320:
Chocolate Research Facility (Singapore).
Designed by Asylum. Photographed by Edwin Tan (Lumina).

INTERIOR POP!
© 2011 an\b editions

First published in Singapore by an\b editions, 2011.
First published in the United States of America by Gingko Press, 2011.

Gingko Press, Inc.
1321 Fifth Street
Berkeley, California 94710, USA
Phone: (510) 898–1195
Fax: (510) 898–1196
books@gingkopress.com
www.gingkopress.com

Publishers: an\b editions. Singapore (www.anb-editions.com)
Publishers: Abdul Nasser and Jacinta Sonja Neoh
Editorial Coordination and Text: Narelle Yabuka
Art Direction and Design: Jacinta Sonja Neoh
Printed by: Tiger Printing (HongKong) Co., Ltd

ISBN: 978-1-58423-399-2

INTERIOR POP!

GINGKO PRESS

contents

foreword

\\\ Images of popular culture were, ironically, an unusual means of creating a new style of art in the 1950s and '60s. Anti-elitist, bold, and highly figurative, pop art was a statement about mass production and consumption. Though it was direct, it was also detached – typically downplaying individualistic expression in favour of an all-encompassing mechanical tone.

In today's digital era, self-expression is within our reach like never before. We can customise our expression of identity at an instantaneous pace, even though the directives and imagery of advertising and mass consumption continue to infiltrate our lives. Keen to attract and maintain our attention in the visual system, the makers of commercial interior spaces are revelling in individualisation through bold art and idiosyncrasy.

The establishments featured in this publication maximise the communicative role of interior design to advertise the products or services offered within them. They do so by creating memorable images and experiences of space through a juxtaposition of two-dimensional visual art and graphics, sculptural installations, and three-dimensional space. *Interior Pop!* surveys how brands and enterprises across the world are using space as their canvas, playing off image and dimension, and making a big impact.

How could one forget the impression of walking inside a 1980s poster, or reclining in a postmodern French salon?

PLAYFUL

giant
surface music
falling to earth
like jewels from the sky

1948

LONDON, UK

design THE WILSON BROTHERS
photos ROGER HARRIS

\\\ Within Nike's 1948 store in London, sporting iconography has been transformed into installation art. Beneath a neon football pitch is an impressively flexible space. Its various elements have been designed with intimate ties to the local neighbourhood, even though the sportswear on sale has global appeal.

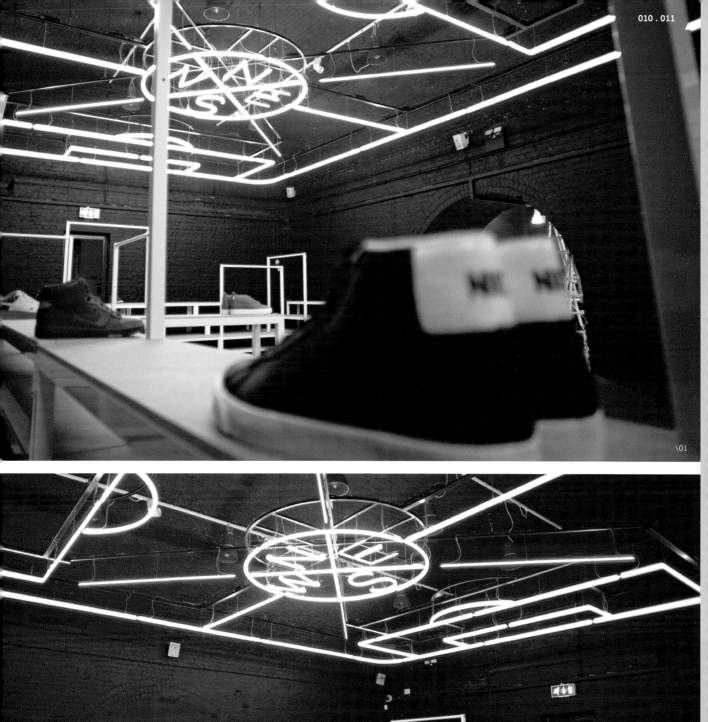

\01

\02

When designing their *Raise Your Game* installation within Nike's 1948 store in Shoreditch, The Wilson Brothers viewed the cavernous space through varied lenses. They envisioned it as a theatre or performance space, and also as a sports field. Beneath blacked-out walls and a vaulted ceiling, they created a playful retail installation that can also stage events.

On the floor they laid Nike GRIND – a rubber sport surface with up to 92% recycled content, a minimum 10% of which is made from the soles of recycled training shoes. The Wilson Brothers calculated that approximately 880 pairs would be smeared across 1948's floor. In homage to the RUN-DEM-CREW, a local urban running club that meets weekly at 1948, the designers installed a "running man" floor graphic that incorporates three maps used by the club. The red (5km), yellow (8km), and green (10km) routes reference local tube lines in the area that are passed on the respective runs, with a visual nod to club founder Charlie Dark's weekly Reggae running podcasts.

A set of twelve modular display units reference tiered stadium or grandstand seating. The steel and laminated plywood units are fitted with wheels and can be quickly re-positioned in new configurations. They are equally useful as displays for merchandise, or as auditorium seating for events. When back-to-back, the stepped units resemble a winners' podium. The hanging rails are detachable and multi-positional, and reference the sea of goal posts at the nearby Hackney Marshes.

\03

\01, 02: A neon ceiling installation lights the cavernous, blacked-out space. A compass is also a reference to the brand and location – Nike Sports Wear (NSW) and East London (E).

\03: Nike GRIND, a rubber sport surface containing the recycled soles of training shoes, was laid on the floor. Graphics pay homage to the routes of a local running group that meets weekly at the store.

\04: The space can be easily reconfigured for fashion events, with the display units able to function as seating. Ample discreet storage space is available in the lowest tier of the display units.

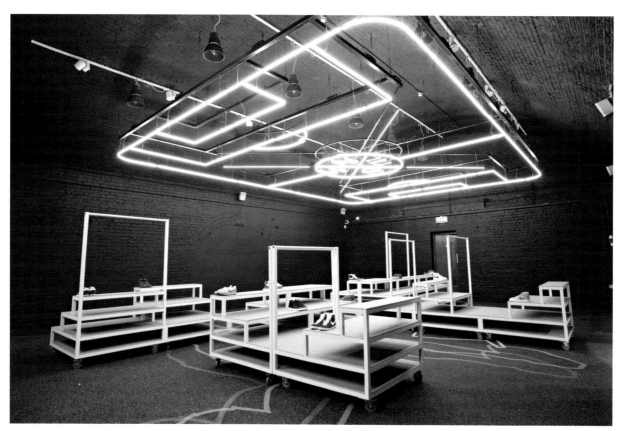

NIKE STADIUM AND PIXARAMIC

LONDON, UK
design THE WILSON BROTHERS
photos LOUISE MELCHIOR

\\\ Nike Stadiums are new multi-purpose brand spaces in London, Berlin, Milan, New York, Paris, and Tokyo that accommodate performances and creative expressions along with sportswear retail. The London incarnation was established at Nike's existing 1948 store. In celebration of its launch, The Wilson Brothers returned with new elements for the space.

The flexibility of The Wilson Brothers' *Raise Your Game* installation at 1948 provided an excellent base for the Nike Stadium experience. Their new work for the store encouraged additional possibilities for interaction with the space and the brand's message. The exterior courtyard that leads to the store entrance was fitted with an illuminated running track and Nike GRIND rubber flooring. The running track encourages interaction and entices customers into the store. It also scales the wall to reach a new neon typographic sign that incorporates 1948's NESW compass.

Just inside the store is PIXARAMIC – a wall cladding system composed of 6,000 manually positioned acrylic cubes. The cubes each have six differently coloured faces – red, green, yellow, blue, black, and white – and their arrangement can be changed to display varied images, statements, and so on. The Wilson Brothers designed the PIXARAMIC system with reference to traditional sporting scoreboards.

New footwear mirrors were also designed for the Nike Stadium experience. A number of these feature programmable LED message boards triggered by proximity sensors. As though whispering the word on the street, the message boards discretely share information about activities and product launches at 1948 in a personalised manner. New modular seating units on lockable castor wheels were inspired by pitch-side dugout areas and offer a comfortable place to try on shoes or hang out.

\02

\03

\04

\01: A new illuminated running track was set into NIKE's recycled rubber flooring at the entry. Neon elements from 1948 were reinforced in signage.

\02: A chrome and glass display cabinet and footwear mirrors display information when activated by customer movement.

\03: A detailed view of the PIXARAMIC wall system reveals the cube colours.

\04: One of the three two-seater modular seating units, which can be moved around the space on castor wheels.

\05: The PIXARAMIC display system can be changed periodically to reflect product launches and promotions.

McDONALD'S McVILLAGE

BARENDRECHT, THE NETHERLANDS

design UXUS
photos DIM BALSEM

\\\ Created predominantly with two-dimensional imagery, McVillage is a playful, educational, and entertaining zone for young children within a McDonald's restaurant in The Netherlands. It contains a series of cottages in which food is traced on its journey from farm to kitchen, and where kids can cook up their own stories.

McDonald's Europe commissioned Dutch design agency UXUS to create an inspiring children's activity area in one of its restaurants in The Netherlands. UXUS was to bring the theme of "what I eat, what I do" to life for kids under seven years of age, and do so in a space no larger than twenty square metres. To maximise the effect within a minimal area, the design team envisaged the project in terms of the spatial application of graphic design.

Large collage-inspired illustrations were created to represent three stages of food production and preparation. The colourful artwork was applied to the floor and wall planes of rooms (or cottages). Within, kids can enjoy simple activities that stimulate their imagination, and cook up their own stories and games. The child's journey starts at the farm, proceeds to the market, and finally ends up at the kitchen. Using both two- and three-dimensional play elements, the child becomes the character in each activity setting: a farmer at the farm (in the fields or on the tractor), a salesperson (at the till) or a shopper (with a trolley) at the market, and a chef in the kitchen (using the blender, cracking an egg, or selecting plates from the cupboard).

The aim was to engage children in a physically playful manner, and communicate a positive message about food in a fun and stimulating way. Special attention was paid to the use of durable and non-toxic materials.

\01: An egg shell chair in the kitchen provides a good spot for relaxing after shopping for food at the adjacent market.

\02: A barn, fields, and sky indicate the farm at the beginning of the McVillage journey.

\03: The market is linked to the farm, where a crop of vegetables emerges from the soil.

\04: Along with the objects represented, differing floor and wall patterns give each area a distinct character.

\05: Plates in the kitchen are mimicked by round mirrors, which lend the space another illusion of depth.

\06: In the market, a child-scaled shopping trolley installation helps kids imagine their selection of foods from stacked shelves.

\07: In the kitchen, children can bounce inside a cushioned capsule that represents a blender.

CHOCOLATE RESEARCH FACILITY

SINGAPORE

design ASYLUM
photos EDWIN TAN (LUMINA)

\\\ The exactitude of science is combined with the pleasure of indulgence at Singapore's Chocolate Research Facility. This laboratory-like chocolate boutique sells one hundred flavours, as well as chocolate-inspired products. Its interior, along with the sweet offerings within, takes obsession and temptation to a whole new level.

Chocolate Research Facility is a Singapore-based chocolate brand and boutique with a number of outlets, one of which is situated within Wheelock Place – an Orchard Road shopping mall. While it promises the pleasures and sweet delights of one hundred flavours of chocolate (including lemongrass, pandan with coconut flake, yam with almond, lychee martini, and lavender), this store makes its unwavering dedication to the chocolate cause resolutely clear.

Design studio Asylum turned the store into a clinical laboratory – a space where pleasure is pursued like a science. An uncompromising cleanliness is its defining factor. Five thousand sterile white tiles were laid both outside and within to reinforce the seriousness with which chocolate is treated here. Bars of chocolate are displayed beneath interrogating lamps for scrutiny through a wide strip window. A storage wall is organised with fanatically labelled boxes in the style of a drugstore or a traditional Chinese medical hall.

No doubt, the attention of passersby is most securely captivated by the indulgent image of litres of melted chocolate dripping down the walls of a storeroom. If Chocolate Research Facility's dedicated customers view this pop-style installation as the altar of Chocolate Research Facility, the holy grail must be the sales counter, which takes the form of an oversized chocolate block.

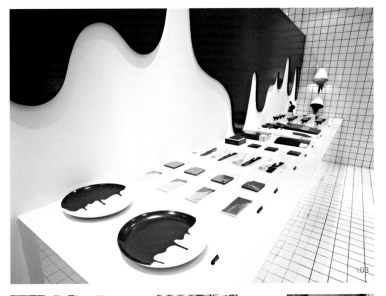

\01: The designers made the most of the corner shop unit with expansive glazing, bold contrasts, and a memorable melted chocolate installation.

\02: An oversized chocolate bar forms the sales counter – a fun interjection within the uncompromising white space.

\03: A variety of chocolate-inspired products are laid out tantalisingly on a reflective bench, which appears to dematerialise.

\04: Asylum also designed the colourful packaging, which focuses attention on the products.

\05, 06: The wide strip window allows the eye-catching products to be scrutinized from the exterior. The long display bench and the clinical white tiles create a laboratory effect.

PLAY AREA AT STINSEN

STOCKHOLM, SWEDEN
design KONCEPT STOCKHOLM
photos MIKAEL FJELLSTRÖM

\\\ A vivid field of artificial grass denotes a popular play area at Stockholm's Stinsen shopping mall. This abstract play landscape allows children to define their own play experiences with the help and company of a family of colourful puppies.

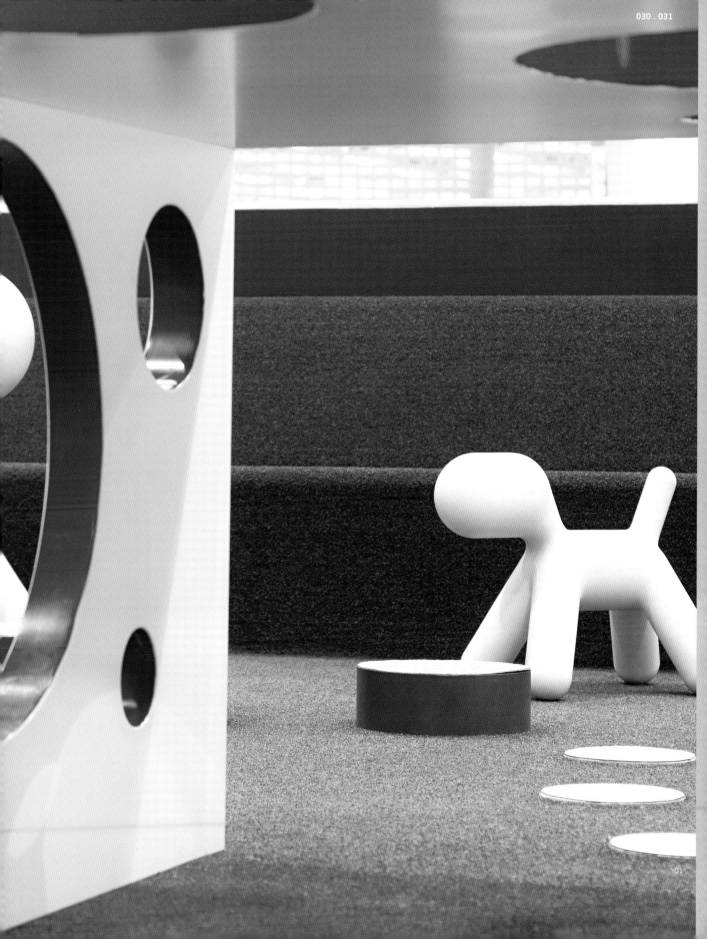

The information age has profoundly affected the way today's children perceive and interact with the world. It has also affected the way they play. Traditional swing-and-slide play sets, for example, have little in common with the non-linear, linked, interactive, and self-determined online world that so shapes the minds of today's young. The play area designed by Koncept Stockholm at the Stinsen shopping mall offers an alternate play experience.

This indoor terrain forgoes typical play equipment in favour of a more abstract play landscape. Children can define their own games and interact with the architectural and landscape elements of the playground itself, as well as with its resident puppies and each other. A pathway is loosely defined with stepping stones on a field of artificial grass. It leads to various play stations including a birch forest, rolling hills, raised pods, and a perforated tunnel. At one end, the grass turns upwards to create a long bench where parents can rest and supervise.

The abstract style that dominates the play landscape allows children to determine how they will use each zone. The colourful plastic dogs (produced by Magis) are popular residents of the space, often being ridden or cared for as if they were pets. The artificial grass provides a comfortable, safe, and sound-absorbing play surface.

\01: A controlled use of colour allows the green grass to be the dominant visual element.

\02: The muted white palette within Stinsen was respected and incorporated into the play area. Small tree houses cantilevered from the birch trunks bring an element of fantasy.

\03: The varied sizes of the puppies lend a surreal tone and encourage imaginative play responses.

\04, 05: The design encourages movement around the space and interaction with each station.

\04

\05

VILASOFA

BARENDRECHT, THE NETHERLANDS

design TJEP.
photos FRANK TJEPKEMA

\\\ Using the iconography of the home, Dutch fast-delivery furniture outlet VilaSofa soothes customers with touches of comfort and familiarity. Conversely, using the iconography of the warehouse, it subtly reminds them that their new sofa is just forty-eight hours away. The playful store design brings new experiences to furniture shopping.

VilaSofa's claim to fame is its promise to deliver its displayed mid-range sofa models to customers' homes within forty-eight hours of purchase. Recognising the nervousness that might accompany such a significant spend, yet wishing to reinforce the brand's point of difference, Dutch design studio Tjep. cleverly mixed the aesthetics of the home and the warehouse to suggest both comfort and speed.

The designers played with concepts and materials related to packaging and delivery – plywood, framing, transportation symbols, bubble wrap, and foam. But these icons have been mixed with reminders of the domestic sphere – balconies, tiles, room-sized display areas, wallpaper, and cut-outs of picture frames, windows, and a giant chandelier.

Picnic benches and tables provide information points at which sales staff can speak dedicatedly with customers. They are adorned by screens that bear the outline of the pitched-roof of an archetypal house. The screens bring the tables into focus within the double-height space. In comparison to the hard-edged benches, the display sofas feel even more comfortable, and this impression is augmented by their enclosure in wall frames that suggest living room proportions. Having made their choice, the customer may remain seated comfortably on their selected sofa while the sales staff wheel over a mobile payment system.

\05

\06

\01: Hazard tape becomes wallpaper and flatness meets perspective. A tile pattern is shown on the floor. A mobile payment trolley can be seen in the corner.

\02, 03: The bright red and pink counteract the more muted colours of the main showroom spaces upstairs, where bold frames divide the volume into domestic-scale rooms and direct movement.

\04: A picnic table serves as a product information point before a playful wall of domestic cut-outs in packing foam white.

\05, 06: A children's slide emerges from a mock window, and chairs can be stacked like packing boxes on a decorated floor.

\07: Bubble wrap becomes the basis for prominent environmental graphics.

ROYAL FLUSH

VALLETTA, MALTA
design CHRIS BRIFFA ARCHITECTS
artwork NORBERT ATTARD
photos CHRIS BRIFFA, NORBERT ATTARD

\\\ The poor state of the public conveniences in the Maltese city of Valletta prompted a radical upgrading proposal from Chris Briffa Architects and the Valletta Local Council. The first of the renovated amenities demonstrates their vision of surprising, art-filled spaces that are unique to their location and encourage people to reconsider their perceptions of the city.

When a youthful new mayor was appointed in
Valleta in 2009, Chris Briffa Architects found a sympathetic
ear for their concerns about the poor state of public toilets
in the city. Discussions concluded that standards must be
raised, but also that a sustainable project for the city should
be developed. The architects embarked on complimentary
design services, imagining Valletta's public conveniences as a
"cultural convenience" – a network of public spaces in which
art would be exhibited.

The idea was rooted in the belief that the restoration
of Valletta (whose buildings date back as far as the
sixteenth century) requires work in both the physical and
psychological realms. Fixing people's perceptions of the city
through their experience of it was considered as important
as physical upgrades. Furthermore, the project aimed to
make contemporary art accessible to sectors of the public
that would not usually attend exhibitions or art museums.

The first amenity to be overhauled is situated in central
Strait Street – the red light district of early 1900s Valletta.
The design theme that modestly frames the venue is that of
a decadent cabaret. A small stage, red lights, and narcissistic
mirrors are joined by an installation from Maltese artist
Norbert Attard titled *V*. Words beginning with "V" form a
veil on the amenities' windows and toggle the mind between
the present and the past life of the location. Inside, a neon
phrase is reflected by mirrors to form a "V" while hinting
at the installations – often considered risqué – that are
produced by a present-day British artist.

\04

\01: The former presence of a cabaret at the site reverberates via faded signage, while the distinct refurbishment presents a thematic interpretation.

\02: Bold red-painted frames surround windows veiled with a series of words that evoke perceptions of the location.

\03: Artist Norbert Attard's reflected neon installation hangs in the entry area above a small curved stage. The cubicles are hidden behind the mirrored wall.

\04: Views of the hand basin area are obscured by additional layers of veiling – translucent white film and playful curtain-shaped mirrors.

\05, 06: The signage for the universal/ women's and men's amenities are small icons cut into the mirrored cubicle doors.

\07: The cubicles, illuminated by white rather than red light, were designed to allow the efficient maintenance required of public conveniences.

\08: Theatrical curtain-shaped mirrors above the hand basins can be detected from the exterior.

\05

\06

\07

\08

RUBY LOUNGE

SYDNEY, AUSTRALIA
design MAKE CREATIVE
photos NICK BOWERS

\\\ Energy, illusion, performance, and fun are aspects of experience that are often sought within nightclubs. At Sydney's Ruby Lounge, interior design sets the stage for an experiential evening in the surrounds of bold graphics, colour contrasts, and a galaxy of overhead mirrors.

A minimal budget was made available to Sydney-based multidisciplinary studio Make Creative for the refurbishment of Ruby Lounge. The space, located on the upper floor of the Eastern Hotel in Bondi Junction, required an entirely new look. The designers developed a lively scheme dominated by high-impact surface treatments that befitted both the budget and the program.

Inspiration was drawn from the optical (op) art movement that was popular in the 1960s. Cleverly making use of optical illusions, works of op art often gave the viewer the impression of movement, warping, and other effects within the picture plane. Make Creative principally favoured the geometric, black-and-white aesthetic common to op art over its visual effects, but an interactive experience is by no means lacking at Ruby Lounge.

The oversized graphics, which were digitally printed on robust vinyl, are reflected in fragments by red-framed ceiling mirrors. This creates lively and changeable impressions of the space, and establishes a strong sense of energy. The mirrors also provide the opportunity for guests to discreetly observe each other. The rear of Ruby was also reconfigured to create an atmospheric lounge space. A collection of glossy black vintage armchairs provides a counterpoint to the new red banquettes that line the lounge area.

\01: Bold op art-inspired graphics are reflected by ceiling mirrors, and red accents speak of the establishment's name.

\02: The quieter lounge area offers ornate and geometric seating, along with a red carpet.

\03: The backlit red bar counter glows seductively. Feature bar lighting was placed with sensitivity to the wall graphics.

\04: A dark base was created for the vibrant graphics with a black ceiling, black-stained floorboards, and black marble cladding on the bar front.

WANDERLUST

SINGAPORE

design ASYLUM, DP ARCHITECTS, FFURIOUS, :PHUNK STUDIO
photos COURTESY OF WANDERLUST (UNLESS OTHERWISE STATED)

\\\ **A world away from Singapore's traditional hotel belts, the Wanderlust boutique hotel is a radical destination for curious voyagers. A team of three Singaporean design agencies and an architecture firm were enlisted to capture the thrill of exploring the world. The result is an eccentric playground in which no two rooms are alike.**

\01

\02

\03

A stay at Wanderlust is akin to an adventure in itself. The hotel is situated within a former school building in Little India – a bustling and colourful area that, according to the hotelier, evades the attention it deserves and warrants discovery. Seeking to attract adventurous spirits, he commissioned a team of designers to create another new world within Wanderlust.

The lobby, designed by Asylum, is themed "Industrial Glam" and juxtaposes the hotel's Little India setting with a more widely recognised aesthetic of concrete, exposed ducts and wiring, and repurposed metal objects. A wall at the entrance features a montage of vintage print advertisements that reflect the neighbourhood's culture. Beyond a rainbow corridor on the second level, :phunk studio created eleven capsule-like rooms and unwaveringly treated each with a single colour. Themed "Eccentricity," each of these rooms contains wall-mounted neon lettering depicting an appropriately themed song title. Thus, "Yellow Submarine," "Purple Haze," and other titles further saturate these immersive spaces.

A change of tone occurs on the third floor, themed "Is It Just Black and White?" DP Architects contrasted a black corridor with nine white rooms that were given either an origami or pop art theme. In the former, sharp undulating ceilings represent paper folds and a lighting systems allows guests to "paint" their room with one of four colours. In the latter, stencil-style installations depict various scenes. fFurious installed a team of friendly monsters on the top floor, inspired by the welcoming gestures of friends abroad. In these loft rooms, themed "Creature Comforts," various creatures offer comfort and companionship.

\04

\05

\01: Asylum's lobby montage of vintage advertisements reflects the culture of Little India. (Image courtesy of Asylum.)

\02: The title of a 1998 album by American psychedelic rock band Yume Bitsu is depicted on the lobby wall. (Image courtesy of Asylum.)

\03: French restaurant Cocotte is situated in the lobby. The space was designed by Asylum. (Image courtesy of Asylum.)

\04: The façade of the 1920s-era school building on Dickson Road remains unchanged.

\05: Asylum's "Industrial Glam" lobby contains furniture made from repurposed urban objects.

\06: In the tree-themed room by fFurious, a tree monster shelters guests with a dense canopy of felt leaves.

\07: A gigantic and surreal typewriter monster, also designed by fFurious, offers cushioned keys as a place to rest.

\08: A wall-bound monster designed by fFurious is composed of printed window blinds and typographic blocks. (Image courtesy of fFurious.)

\09: A curious monster inhabits a floor feature of mosaic tiles in a spaceship-themed room designed by fFurious. (Image courtesy of fFurious.)

\10: A galaxy of stars sets the scene for the spaceship-themed room by fFurious.

\11, 12: Two of DP Architects' third floor pop art-inspired rooms that mix real and depicted domestic items.

\13–18: :phunk studio designed the single-colour rooms on the second level. Each room is named with reference to a song title – thus, "My White Noise" (13), "Yellow Submarine" (14), "Pink Triangle" (15), "Blue Order" (16), "Purple Haze" (17), and "Red Light" (18).

POP-UP STORE FOR STELLA McCARTNEY

PARIS, FRANCE
design GILES MILLER
photos RICHARD CORCORAN

\\\ A historic textile pattern, the bold sculptures of the pop art movement, high-end fashion retailing, and a low-cost throwaway material came head-to-head in Paris at the Pop-Up Store for Stella McCartney. The various qualities of humble corrugated cardboard were explored and manipulated for the creation of this transportable and recyclable installation.

British designer Giles Miller has experimented with corrugated cardboard for several years, developing products and surface finishes, and manipulating the material for commissioned work. His exploratory approach has resulted in the design of objects such as a cardboard handbag, grandfather clock, lamp, bench, martini glass, wardrobe, and screen, among other items.

Miller has undertaken several projects for fashion designer Stella McCartney, one of which is a bold pop-up shop for the Galeries Lafayette department store on Boulevard Hausmann in Paris. Making use of corrugated cardboard's lightness, sheet size, strength, and texture, he created an installation that included giant three-dimensional cardboard letters spelling "Stella." The letters ranged in height from one and a half metres to two metres, and were placed in a staggered manner that challenged how one read and gauged perspective.

Miller also created a series of richly textured display cubes for the store, which cleverly exploited the decorative potential of corrugated cardboard's fluted inner layer. The chequered pattern of cardboard squares was established by arranging squares of laminated sheets that were sliced through at different angles. After its showing in Paris, the installation was flown to London, where it was displayed in Selfridges on Oxford Street.

\01, 02: Humble cardboard made a pronounced display in the exclusive surrounds of the Galeries Lafayette.

\03, 04: The use of one material across the installation brought cohesion and a strong singular expression to both identity and display elements.

\05: The structure and stability of the cubes was established by an internal layer of flat cardboard sheets.

\06: The human scale of the letters created a playful, rather than daunting, atmosphere for shopping.

\07, 08, 09: The decorative possibilities of fluting were explored and developed into a chequered pattern.

\10: Gold leaf was applied to the faces of the display cubes.

\03

\04

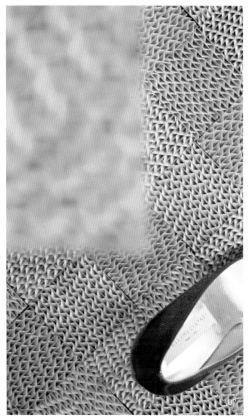

\05

\07

\09

\06

\08

\10

TICKET

STOCKHOLM, SWEDEN
design BVD, KONCEPT STOCKHOLM
photos PATRIK LINDELL

\\\ A substantial share of the ticketing market for private travel has shifted to Internet-based sales in recent years. Competition between travel agencies for the remaining customer group has thus increased markedly. In response, Swedish travel agency Ticket sought ways to encourage customer loyalty through branding and interior design.

Facing competitive business conditions, Ticket realised that their existing store designs no longer adequately communicated their competitive advantages, such as knowledge, service, and a wide range of offers. They commissioned design and branding agency BVD and spatial design studio Koncept Stockholm to develop a new shop concept for Ticket and the first pilot shop in Sollentuna Centrum in Stockholm.

The new concept focuses on generating an emotive response from the customer – the feeling of excitement and buzz that comes with one's purchase of a travel ticket or one's arrival at the airport. Ticket's corporate colour – a dark shade of red – was made brighter and more energetic, and applied to furniture, signage, and other graphics. New counters were designed to reduce the distance between customers and sales staff, and increase the feeling of personal contact, immediacy, and openness.

The typography and graphic symbols adopted are similar to those found at airports. Lively dotted lines were playfully applied to the floor (in a manner akin to runway markings), to the walls (in a crisscrossed configuration reminiscent of flight paths), and to internal windows. Ticket's vibrant store graphics take precedence over airline and tour company logos, which are rendered in pale grey. The customer's focus, therefore, is continually directed towards their upcoming adventure, and Ticket's provision of service.

\01: A staggered shelf design directs the eyes all around the display.

\02: Distinct red graphics and furniture capture attention and communicate the excitement of travel.

\03: Typography and graphic symbols are similar to those found at airports.

\04: Floor graphics are reminiscent of airport runway markings and cast the customer's mind to their upcoming travel experience.

\05: The new counters reduce the distance between customers and sales staff, and bear resemblance to airport check-in counters.

STYLE CLUB

DUBLIN, IRELAND

design company DOUGLAS WALLACE ARCHITECTS
AND DESIGNERS (NOW DW-SQUARED)
designer GARRY COHN/HUGH WALLACE
photos CONOR HORGAN

\\\ **Imagine if you could take aesthetic elements from punk, Japanimation, new wave, Memphis, and traditional upholstery, churn them in a blender, and have fun with the leftover pieces. You would probably end up with something like Style Club – a concept salon in Dublin for those who like to be daring with their hair.**

\01

The Alice in Wonderland metaphor is often used to describe places that seem deliberately nonsensical. In the case of Style Club, says designer Garry Cohn for Douglas Wallace Architects and Designers (now dw-squared), Alice would be a punk rocker. In this adventurous concept salon, patterns clash, colours collide, and shapes and forms are placed in strange combinations. The salon owner, Mark Keaveney of Peter Mark, asked Douglas Wallace Architects and Designers to provide a cutting-edge interior that would alter how hair salons are perceived. With a mixed bag of references and a postmodern perspective, Cohn provided an imaginative design that draws mixed reactions.

From the street, one can glimpse vibrant salmon-coloured walls contrasting with traditional white mouldings beneath a wildly patterned lenticular (three-dimensional graphic) ceiling. Beyond, a waiting area – with traditional-style upholstery on seating as well as ceiling panels – beckons unusually. A wall of convex mirrors against a stripe-patterned wall sits next to a tartan wall, next to blue stylised clouds, beneath a pink giraffe-skin printed ceiling.

The styling stations in the centre of the space adopt candy colours and chunky geometric shapes. Stretching right through the salon is a runway of sorts. Its tiles were laser cut to achieve a stylised pattern of hair clippings. The green-tinged bathroom is swathed in grass-print tiles. Above a green toilet hangs artwork in which an inquisitive cow peers into the room.

\02

\03

\01: On a wall of reflections, convex mirrors and lights surround flat mirrors at eye height and create a dizzying array of views.

\02: The century-old building is listed as a Dublin landmark, and required restoration work both externally and internally to reinstate its original condition. An addition was created at the rear.

\03: Upholstery dominates the reception area, in which shiny white fabric-covered ceiling panels hover over a reception desk upholstered with silver fabric, an over-sized red velvet sofa, and a 1980s-style coffee bar.

\04: A catwalk of laser-cut tiles represents hair clippings on the floor.

\05: A pink giraffe-patterned ceiling caps an intensely patterned area that contains the chunky, vividly coloured styling stations. Furniture was designed and selected to impart a bold character.

\06, 08, 09: A collage of shapes, colours, and patterns enlivens the shampooing area.

\07: A collection of TV screens, some of which are tipped sideways, comically layers image upon image to almost illegible ends.

\10: Two and three dimensions were combined.

\11: In the bathroom, grass-print tiles seemingly entice a cow that peers in through a mock window. Green sanitaryware was installed.

VIRGIN HOLIDAYS V-ROOM

LONDON, UK

interior design W1 STUDIO
graphic design HAWAII DESIGN
photos TOBY SUMMERSKILL

\\\ Implicit in the sale of holiday packages is the promise of leisure and pleasure – of time out, exploration, play, and relaxation. Virgin Holidays perceived the potential for reinforcing the holiday buzz within v-room – its Gatwick Airport departure lounge. Three-dimensional installations and two-dimensional artwork were employed to create an engaging and exciting departure experience.

Specifically catering to Virgin Holidays customers, the v-room departure lounge was designed by W1 Studio and Hawaii Design to impart a clubhouse experience. W1 Studio managed the project and conceived the interior design, and Hawaii Design was asked to contribute an exciting and engaging visual environment. The v-room was to make customers feel special and help initiate the feeling of being on holiday. Specific areas were to appeal to particular age groups (for instance, the adults-only quiet area, the children's play room, and the Internet and games room), but all had to be original and fun.

The main room required an installation that appealed to all ages. Virgin Holidays requested the presence of a world map in the space, and Hawaii Design devised a reinterpretation that could maximise the map's appeal across age groups. They created an installation of objects rather than a typical printed map. The map was made with shapes representing paper aeroplanes – suitable in theme, and common to many childhoods. Each aeroplane was injected-moulded and screwed to the wall individually.

The Internet and games room contains computer terminals and fussball tables (for table-top football). Hawaii Design wished to include something tactile and interactive as a counterpoint to the distant digital world. A spinning wall of 1,452 fussball players was created – a clever way to contrast technology with a tactile, low-tech, fun, and interactive reference.

\02

\01: A wall of spinning fussball players establishes a fun theme within the Internet and games room. Red and white figures were chosen to reinforce Virgin's corporate colours.

\02: Using a muted black and white palette, as well as a variety of figures, shapes, and words at various heights, artwork in the café area was designed to appeal to a wide range of ages.

\03: A world map installation features injection-moulded plastic planes. A number of planes are suspended from the waved ceiling as though in flight.

\04: An abstract atmospheric graphic was applied to the glass partitions that enclose the children's play room.

\05: The map installation of injection-moulded planes creates varying shadows during the day.

\03

\04

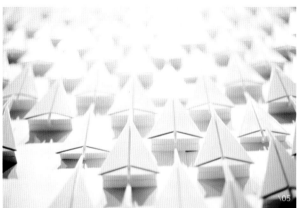

\05

POP
FASHION
STORE

MUNICH, GERMANY

design EXPOLAB ADVANCED COMMUNICATION AND DESIGN
photos MAREK VOGEL, PAT KALT

\\\ The atmosphere of a nightclub and the essence
of 'pop' were sought during the design of POP
Fashion Store in Munich. The influence of pop art
and comics meets meticulous surface design in
this space of contrasts and quirks. A sense of the
mechanical (rather than the organic) pervades, just
as it did in the earliest works of pop art.

How might the term 'pop' be interpreted these days? The team at EXPOLAB Advanced Communication and Design grappled with this question when designing POP Fashion Store – a streetwear boutique on Sendlinger Strasse in Munich. They determined that the idiosyncratic character of POP (the store) and 'pop' (the concept) was best demonstrated by clean surfaces, graphic contrasts, a deliberate use of colour, and quirky details.

With the store's youthful demographic in mind, EXPOLAB set about establishing a nightclub atmosphere with glossy black surfaces and vivid green highlights. A generous two-level floor area encouraged the development of club-like zones for overlooking, gathering, and flaunting. Display furniture was designed with energetic slants and cantilevers, and colourful artwork was boldly applied to black walls. The payment counter and cash register were given the form of a giant gorilla sawn in half, which has become known as the 'King of POP' and the store mascot.

The desired expression of energy, clarity, colour, and contrasts is perhaps most succinctly embodied in the custom-made light installation, titled *Rush of Lights*. This overhead current is composed of strands of self-luminous, multi-coloured optical fibre. Two kilometres of cable were used, and the installation appears to extend to infinity through the use of mirrors. *Rush of Lights* pulsates to music with the help of different programming modules.

\01: A dramatically cantilevering ledge makes a gesture of movement and flow.

\02: The store has two entrances, and mirrored surfaces behind a shoe display reflect the activity that occurs outside one of them.

\03: An expressive gorilla makes an unusual payment counter and a memorable store mascot.

\04, 05: Mirrored surfaces reflect the *Rush of Lights* installation. Its pulsating coloured light matches the rhythm of the music played in the store.

\06: The fitting room walls and doors feature pop-style artwork that defies any form in particular.

\04

\05

\06

ILLUSIONARY

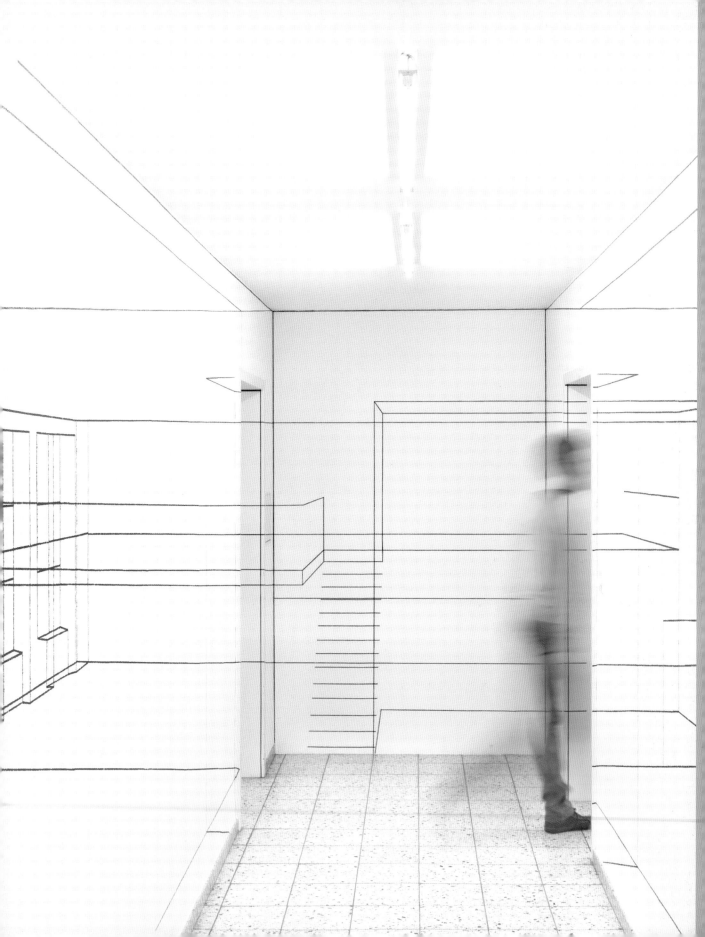

EMPEROR MOTH

LONDON, UK
design AB ROGERS DESIGN
photos MORLEY VON STERNBERG

\\\ Stepping off London's Mount Street into the Emperor Moth boutique is like journeying from "Old England" into some electrified future realm. The dynamic Russian fashion label's fragmented, mirrored retail space is full of movement and vivid colours. It gives the impression of being everywhere, but nowhere at the same time.

Emperor Moth approached Ab Rogers Design (ARD) for the creation of a new retail space in London's Mayfair that would be representative of the vivid colours and dynamism of the brand – a space that would feel alive and full of movement. The resulting space shatters the charm of the gentile Mount Street environment, its window displays exploding into the street context and contaminating the outside world with energy, life, and excitement.

The boutique is split over two floors – a ground level retail space and a basement for VIPs. ARD drew inspiration from French sculptor Nikki de Saint Phalle's Tarot Garden and the mirror work of American artist Robert Smithson to create a voluptuous internal space dominated by a multi-faceted mirrored tent. The mirrored skin engulfs the shop space. Its multi-directional fragments give the customer the feeling of being everywhere in the shop, and yet nowhere at once. The blue floor compounds the atmospheric effect. It was inspired by the sea and the sky, and provides a calming backdrop.

ARD played further with impressions of reality by hanging puppet-like mannequins in the space, and transforming clothes hangers into heads. Inspiration was drawn from historical puppet culture – from Pinocchio to *Being John Malkovich*. ARD viewed puppetry as a way of taking inhuman-looking objects and making them seem alive. The puppets in the dynamic Emperor Moth environment are yet another pulse of energy and excitement.

\06

\01: The mirrored surface acts like a
tent – a skin that engulfs the shop space.
Mannequins were given puppet-like bodies
to imply that they could spring to life at
any moment.

\02: The "Old English" charm of Mayfair
is shattered by the riotous energy of
Emperor Moth.

\03: Clothes hangers take on a vibrant,
animate dimension.

\04: The store interior is representative
of the vivid colours and dynamism of the
Emperor Moth brand.

\05: The fragmented, mirrored surface
stretches from the ground level space
down to the VIP basement area.

\06: Vibrant pink strips bring an electrified
quality to the space, while the blue floor
creates a calming backdrop.

THE CAFETERIA OF THE PALAZZO DELLE ESPOSIZIONE

VENICE, ITALY
design TOBIAS REHBERGER
furniture ARTEK
photos WOLFGANG GÜNZEL, KATJA HAGELSTAM

\\\ At the Venice Biennale's 53rd International Art Exhibition, cafeteria-goers became performers in a functional sculpture. German artist Tobias Rehberger collaborated with Artek to produce a mesmerising domain using geometric forms and contrasting colours. Art became spatial in this complex environment, which was inspired by the dazzle painting once applied to warships.

As a sponsor of the 53rd International Art Exhibition at La Biennale di Venezia, furniture company Artek collaborated with several artists to produce a cafeteria, a bookshop, and an educational area. The Venice Biennale Foundation had aimed to strengthen the interdisciplinary nature of the International Art Exhibition, and dialogue between art and architecture was one of the means through which it wished to do so. Tobias Rehberger's cafeteria established a deep conversation between the two disciplines.

Rehberger drew inspiration from the dazzle painting that was applied to navy ships for camouflage during the First World War. Rather than conceal ships, the bold, highly visible, and clashing patterns of dazzle painting created confusion by impeding the effectiveness of the visual rangefinders on enemy vessels. Dazzle painting made it difficult for rangefinder operators to bring an image of a ship into focus, and thus deciphering its position and direction became problematic.

In the spatial environment of the cafeteria, Rehberger's clashing stripes and patterns, contrasting colours, and intersecting shapes created visual disorientation. Using paint and Artek furniture – both whole pieces and refashioned parts – Rehberger blurred the perceived distinction between planes and volumes. Walls appeared to bend, furniture seemed to disappear or jump into view, and one's ability to focus on particular elements was often undermined. Cafeteria-goers became performers in this functional sculpture, as their eyes navigated for focal points in a complex environment.

\02

\03

\05

\06

\07

\08

\09

\10

\01: Fragmented and layered patterns, along with unusual furniture shapes, served to undermine one's ability to focus on particular objects or planes.

\02: Outdoor signage for the cafeteria.

\03: Painted Alvar Aalto furniture was mixed with abstract pieces assembled by Rehberger using parts of Aalto's furniture. A composition of facetted mirrors behind the bar counter adds to the dazzling effect.

\04, 05: Ducts were employed as sculptural objects, and hinted at the maritime context in which dazzle painting was previously used.

\06: Seemingly precarious, an angular shade structure stood over the outdoor seating area, where the complex colour patterns were continued.

\07, 08: A complex scheme of geometric forms and contrasting colours created a visually disorienting, collaged environment.

\09, 10: Two and three dimensions were made to interact and spatial distinctions were blurred by a complex pattern of paint.

ANNA

BASEL, SWITZERLAND
design ZMIK
photos EIK FRENZEL

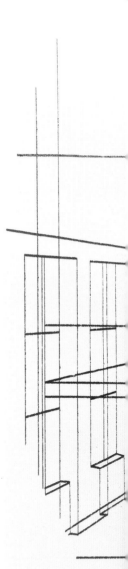

\\\ An anamorphic intervention titled *ANNA* disrupts and enlivens one's experience of a narrow and generic corridor in a Basel office building. Simultaneously, it speaks of the interactive nature of the work produced there.

iart interactive is a digital design agency based in Basel whose work straddles media, art, and technology. The agency designs lighting, projection, and interaction solutions for museums, exhibitions, architectural projects, public spaces, and media-based artworks. It is fitting, therefore, that iart interactive's own office offers an interactive experience. This takes the form of a corridor intervention created by spatial design studio ZMIK and titled *ANNA*.

ZMIK's intervention was prompted by the relocation of iart interactive's office to a 1970s-era building. ZMIK visually enlarged the main circulation area – a generic narrow, tiled corridor – using the technique of anamorphosis. A set of wireframe drawings were applied to the corridor walls, and depending on the viewer's position, they appear as either abstract markings or perspective drawings.

When viewed in five particular directions from three fixed positions, the drawings show real and imaginary rooms behind the walls. The implied fictional rooms extend the real ones to create a wider spatial perspective. The drawings were created by transferring projected vector drawings onto the walls using black markers. iart interactive regards the intervention as an allegory for the quest for new perspectives.

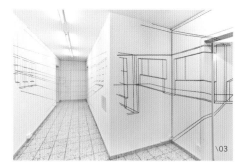

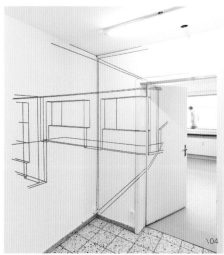

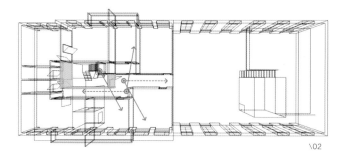

\01: The confines of a bare, narrow corridor are broken by a visual extension of the space.

\02: An exploded plan drawing shows the positions and directions for viewing, as well as the real spaces (to the left) and the fictional depicted spaces (to the right).

\03, 04: Perspective drawings appear and dissolve as one moves through the corridor.

\05: Vivid paint on the stairwell enclosure lends a green glow to the surrounding white walls.

\06: When not viewed from the fixed positions, the lines appear as abstract markings.

\05

\06

ZAHA HADID AND SUPREMATISM

ZURICH, SWITZERLAND
design ZAHA HADID ARCHITECTS
photos MARTIN RUETSCHI

\\\ Both an exhibition and a site-specific artwork, *Zaha Hadid and Suprematism* transformed Zurich's Galerie Gmurzynska into a spatial painting. This seminal show juxtaposed the works of the early-twentieth-century Russian avante garde with that of Zaha Hadid, who curated and designed the exhibition with partner Patrik Schumacher. The warped and anti-gravitational space of the Russian paintings was expressed spatially by Hadid, who encouraged an interactive experience of the exhibition.

The work of architect Zaha Hadid took its initial inspiration from the Russian avante-garde artists of the early twentieth century. A particular influence was the abstract work of suprematist artist Kasimir Malevich, which informed Hadid's graduation project in the 1970s. With painted compositions of squares, rectangles, triangles, and circles, Malevich sought to capture movement and the feeling of colour in space – to free his art from the weight of the real world. Similarly, Hadid's work seeks fluid spaces and a denial of solidity.

The exhibition *Zaha Hadid and Suprematism* translated the Russian avante-garde paintings and sculptures of Malevich, El Lissitzky, and Alexander Rodchenko into Hadid's own architectural language. The architect warped one's perception of the gallery interior with a bold black-and-white spatial painting that expanded the picture plane into habitable space. A strong juxtaposition was established with the colourful suprematist paintings.

Hadid choreographed the gallery space into zones that focused on four themes – abstraction, distortion, fragmentation, and floatation. Artwork was grouped according to these themes. As visitors studied the clusters of framed suprematist work, they also experienced the dynamic visual and spatial interventions of Hadid, who translated the warped and anti-gravitational space of the Russian art into her own architectural language.

\02

\03

\04

\05

\06

\07

\08

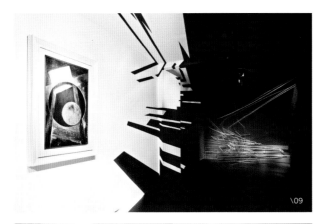

\09

\10

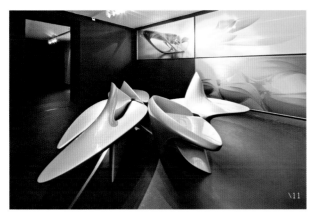

\11

\12

\01: Paintings by Paul Mansouroff and Kasimir Malevich were juxtaposed with Hadid's perspective-bending relief and wire frame sculpture.

\02, 03: Viewed from the footpath through a large window, Hadid's artwork encouraged a warped spatial reading of the gallery interior.

\04: A drawing indicating Hadid's spatial painting.

\05, 06: Hadid's *Great Utopia Clusters* faced a painting by Malevich. The gallery was transformed into an interactive three-dimensional painting.

\07: *Zephyr Sofa, Crater Table,* and drawings by Hadid.

\08: Paintings by El Lissitzky, Alexander Rodchenko, Ilya Chashnik, and Nikolai Suetin were hung near Hadid's *Seoul Desk.*

\09: A painting by Rodchenko and the *Victoria City Wire Frame* sculpture by Hadid.

\10: Hadid's *Silver Models.*

\11: Works from Hadid's *Silver Paintings* series and her Orchis outdoor stools.

\12: Hadid's *Lunar Triptych Relief.*

REEBOK
FLASH

NEW YORK, USA
design FORMAVISION
photos JORDAN KLEINMAN

\\\ **Open for just one month in New York, Reebok's first ever pop-up store presented a flashback to the 1980s with relaunched sneaker lines and exclusive artist collaborations. Reebok Flash immersed shoppers in a dynamic retail environment as well as into the pop spirit of the '80s.**

Befitting its short life span, little more than paint was used to craft Reebok's first pop-up store. However, the medium was well chosen and deftly handled by experimental design studio Formavision. The temporary retail space was located within a New York gallery, which itself lies within a warehouse building. In this context of art and shifting goods, Formavision mixed 1980s cultural cues with the principles of visual abstraction used by British vorticist artists of the early twentieth century.

Provocative and confounding, the interior captured the thrill of pop-up shopping and was an ideal advertisement for the products within. Reebok Flash marketed limited-edition sneakers and apparel collections designed in collaboration with visual artists Rolland Berry, John Maeda, and the estate of Jean-Michel Basquiat. It also relaunched several of the company's most poplar sneaker lines from the 1980s, including Pump and the Freestyle series.

Formavision mixed iconographic shapes from Reebok sneakers (such as stripes and hexagons) with an '80s pop culture aesthetic that recalled the colours and forms of *Miami Vice, Flashdance, Thriller,* and *Purple Rain*. Choreographed colour blocks and angled display boxes tricked the eye, playing with one's sense of depth and perspective. The result was a space that immersed shoppers as though they had stepped into a poster.

\03

\02

\04

\05

\06

\07

\08

\09

\01: The horizontal floor appeared wildly warped, and display surfaces took on precarious leans.

\02: Digital renderings – an exploded plan view and two wall elevations – aided the design process.

\03: A neon nod to Reebok's British heritage took a lightning bolt angularity at the counter.

\04: Confounding one's sense of perspective, three-dimensional shapes extended into distorted graphic patterns in an impressive visual manipulation of depth.

\05: Reebok logos and slogans were made part of the graphic composition.

\06: Fragments of mirror brought another visual layer and, at the same time, reinforced the unpredictability of pop-up shopping.

\07: Stripes appeared to flatten out a corner, but a difference in wall height deliberately undermined the visual trickery.

\08: Floor, wall, and display platform appeared to merge at a rear corner.

\09: A 3D rendering of the stairs reveals the complexity of the design.

WOMEN'S AMENITIES, V&A MUSEUM

LONDON, UK

interior design GLOWACKA RENNIE ARCHITECTS
artwork FELICE VARINI
photos ANTHONY WELLER
(ARCHIMAGE ARCHITECTURAL PHOTOGRAPHY)

\\\ The Women's Amenities that service the Grand Entrance hall at the Victoria and Albert (V&A) Museum in London are as much a gallery as a restroom. Designed with respect to the museum's intent to raise standards in and promote the fine and decorative arts, the impeccably crafted amenities incorporate jewel-like fittings and artwork that reveals itself as one experiences the space.

The Grand Entrance to the V&A Museum on London's Cromwell Road forms an important arrival point for visitors to the museum, as well as a venue for major V&A events and parties. The grand, domed, marbled space imparts an impression of grandeur and refinement. Keen to further refine the experience of its visitors, the museum instigated an invited design competition for the refurbishment of the attached women's amenities.

Glowacka Rennie Architects were awarded the commission with a refined scheme incorporating a painted installation by Swiss artist Felice Varini. The designers established a new stone datum – a heavy base that unifies the space with the descending staircase through which it is accessed. Above this datum, a ribbed, vaulted ceiling ripples in accordance with the rhythm of existing windows. Against the muted palette of dark and pale stone and light-coloured finishes, brass fittings and trims stand out like jewellery.

Varini's installation is true to the style of the geometric, perspective-localised paintings for which he is known. His fragments of blue lines reveal themselves as a composition of interlocking circles when one looks into the basin mirror. For the museum visitor, the amenities provide the satisfying experience of participating in a surprising creative work, while also functioning as a comfortable and elegant facility.

\02

\03

\04

\05

\01: A combination of dark and pale stone creates a heavy-looking base. Varini's composition begins to reveal itself as the cubicles are approached.

\02: The ribs, along with the painted blue lines, are partially visible as one descends from the Grand Entrance hall to the Women's Amenities.

\03: When one looks into the basin mirror, the perspective-localised painting of interlocking circles snaps into alignment.

\04: A system of ribs creates a vaulted ceiling that exaggerates the generous height of the space. Felice Varini's artwork is an intriguing overlay of blue lines.

\05: Against the muted backdrop, brass fittings take on a jewel-like quality.

\06: Fragments of the dancing ceiling are visible from each cubicle.

\06

KANTAR JAPAN RECEPTION

TOKYO, JAPAN

design KWAS (KENSUKE WATANABE ARCHITECTURE STUDIO)
photos MASAMI DAITO

\\\ In many office receptions, the visitor merely plays a subservient role – by seeking the guidance of a receptionist. At Kantar Japan, however, the visitor is an active participant in a surprising reception experience – discovering, navigating, and using (in whichever way they determine) a complex geometric sculpture.

Kantar Japan is a company that translates information into insights that inspire its clients to make creative business decisions. It provides assistance with branding, ad testing, demand forecasting, product development, and sales support for a wide range of industries that range from food and beverage, to cosmetics, jewellery, electrical goods, financial products, and IT products, among others.

The company recently shifted its headquarters to a tower in Tokyo's Shinjuku area. kwas was engaged to develop a reception area and used the concept of inspiration – a key goal of Kantar Japan – to shape a memorable installation. Although the resulting reception area is sufficiently abstract to favour no particular industry over others, it is also affecting enough to create a lasting impression.

The installation is read as a perfect yellow "K" from the point at which the visitor enters the room. As the visitor approaches, however, the composition of the "K" gradually transforms and shows a different appearance. It is revealed to be a series of apparently unrelated objects that have been appropriately scaled for use as benches or display platforms.

\03

\04

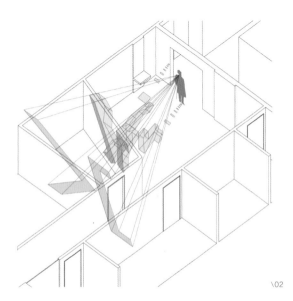

\02

\01: In the dark grey reception area, the yellow elements make a distinct impression.

\02: An axonometric drawing indicates the point from which one sees a perfect K.

\03, 04: From a particular position at the entrance, the abstract yellow elements align to form a "K" and show the company logo. The "K" (composed of a square bracket and an arrow) is always presented with a scale of yellow marks and appears at the point in a document or on screen where the reader will find inspirational information.

\05, 06: One's interaction with the yellow objects can extend to seating and the display of items.

116 , 117
Kantar Japan K

Japan Kantar Research
TNS Infoplan
Kantar Express
Kantar Retail
(Glendinning Japan)

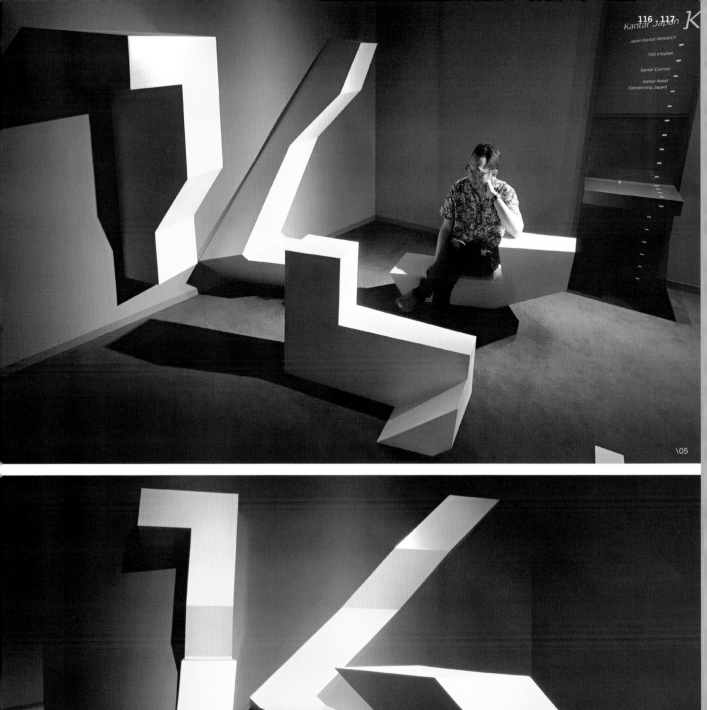

\05

\06

LEO BURNETT OFFICE

SINGAPORE

design MINISTRY OF DESIGN
photos CI&A PHOTOGRAPHY

\\\ American advertising legend Leo Burnett believed that big ideas come out of big pencils. A portrait of the man himself (along with a very large pencil) greets visitors to the agency's Singapore office. Graphic elements and sculptural installations abound at this quirky workplace, reflecting the spirit of transformative creativity that lives on in the agency.

Leo Burnett (1891–1971) was one of America's most highly regarded advertising executives, having developed some of that country's (and the world's) most recognisable brand mascots. His agency lives on with a network of offices around the world. The Singapore branch, with a staff of 112, enjoys a space designed by Ministry of Design that incorporates three environments – "space to impress, space to interact, and space to create."

The lift lobby and reception area compose the first of these zones. The portrait of Burnett, which boldly welcomes those exiting the lift, is over three metres in height. It was painted directly onto the floor, walls, windows, and ceiling with energetic brush strokes that speak of the personality and the work he produced. The second zone, "space to interact," is comprised of breakout and meeting spaces that allow for gatherings of various types. Illuminated by a spotlight, a wheelbarrow full of trophies makes an unusual installation in the chill-out area. Vivid green meeting rooms can be glimpsed through portholes in a muted black corridor.

An open-plan work area forms the third zone – "space to create." The energetic vibe of the public areas is continued with playful customised desks. The plywood tabletops were stained to a variety of shades and arranged in a chequered pattern. An outdoor deck area is hemmed by the black paint strokes that compose an anamorphic art feature – a fifteen-metre-long figure "7+" that represents the agency's aspired internal project rating benchmark.

\02

\03

\04

"When you reach for the stars you may not quite get one, but you won't come up with a handful of mud either."

\06

\07

\08

\01: In the main entry foyer, creative possibilities are suggested by the over-scaled pencil that trails mid-stroke from a portrait of Leo Burnett.

\02: An anamorphic artwork hems an informal outdoor deck area and reminds staff of the agency's aspiration for high achievement.

\03: In the work area, stained custom-made desks are arranged in a chequered pattern. Hotdesks are placed at the periphery.

\04: The office is located in a preserved building on Murray Street, near Chinatown in central Singapore.

\05: A cool white reception counter is adorned by a bowl of apples, echoing the bowl that famously took a place in Burnett's first office.

\06: The office's trophies are stockpiled and spotlighted in the chill-out area.

\07: Digital media brings further energy to the space. A wall-sized projection canvas enhances the chill-out area and embedded screens display the agency's past work on the reception counter.

\08: The red apple has played a key role in Leo Burnett's history and branding. Apples in a feature wall were individually decorated by staff members.

\09–11: The meeting rooms are vividly coloured, and can be glimpsed through portholes in a mysterious black corridor.

ILLUSTRATIVE

BOSS ORANGE (SPECIAL CONCEPT STORE)

SHANGHAI, CHINA
graphic design PROJEKTTRIANGLE DESIGN STUDIO
interior design RAISERLOPES ARCHITECTS//INTERIOR ARCHITECTS
photos TOM ZIORA

\\\ A delicate graphic sensibility meets a robust architectural style in the special concept store for BOSS Orange in Shanghai. The brand offers a more youthful, casual, and street-friendly line of clothing than its well-known German parent HUGO BOSS. Accordingly, an exploratory graphic theme was developed for the global Orange campaign.

BOSS Orange presents itself as an unconventional leisurewear label – as one that takes a playful approach to proportions, mixes materials, and contrasts colours and patterns experimentally. Naturally, expressing this in its store interiors is an important means of communicating the brand's approach, and differentiating it from the higher-end HUGO BOSS line. The BOSS Orange Special Concept Store in Shanghai embodies the worldwide in-store graphics campaign developed by Projekttriangle Design Studio for the brand.

RAISERLOPES architects//interior architects established a robust interior environment of raw pine, concrete, steel, exposed light bulbs, and muted hues. Compounding the impression of experimentation and work in progress, Projekttriangle layered on whimsical graphics with a hand-drawn quality. The graphic concept was themed "Good old Germany." A nostalgic, dream-like, fairy tale atmosphere was initiated, and with a focus on imagery of flora and fauna, Projekttriangle explored typical German icons such as songbirds.

A veritable aviary of birds graces the interior. A traditional wood and rubber stamp set was produced, consisting of ten typical German songbirds in life size. The stamps were applied by hand onto objects, walls, and shelves. Also developed was a six-metre-high "fantasy tree," which was illustrated by hand and later screen-printed onto the timber.

\02

\03

\04

\05

\06

\07

\01, 06, 09, 11: Originally drawn by
hand, a "fantasy tree" was screen-printed
onto raw timber. It is populated by
German songbirds.

\02: The "fantasy tree" is also expressed
at the shop front, where the installation
of unfinished timber shelves and boxes is
made apparent.

\03, 04: Knitted wire forms a decorative
balustrade. A wall of songbirds,
individually stamped by hand, depicts
them at life size.

\05: A gigantic songbird mural dominates
a wall, hinting at calligraphic brush
strokes and the Chinese context. Classic
German-designed chairs reinforce the
heritage of the HUGO BOSS brand.

\07: A timber detail depicts the name of
a German castle.

\08: Lacquered surfaces bring a smoother
touch to the change rooms, and over-sized
birds keep watch.

\10: A small bird application on a mirror.

BOSS ORANGE (FLAGSHIP STORE)

MANNHEIM, GERMANY
graphic design PROJEKTTRIANGLE DESIGN STUDIO
interior design BLOCHER BLOCHER SHOPS
photos THOMAS MARDO

\\\ As part of its on-going collaboration with HUGO BOSS, Projekttriangle Design Studio was engaged for the design of interior graphics for the BOSS Orange flagship store in Mannheim, Germany. A whimsical, nostalgic graphic theme dominates, and a collection of fantastical creatures dwells within the space.

The graphic campaign developed by Projekttriangle Design Studio for BOSS Orange stores across the world is one that can be readily developed and abstracted. At the flagship store in Mannheim, it took on new forms. It was reconsidered to suit the particularities of the three-storey space, in which interior designers Blocher Blocher Shops had created a muted palette and manipulated the brand's display direction.

The centrepiece of the Mannheim store is a twelve-metre-high wall installation – a "fantasy tree" on which elaborately drawn rabbits, squirrels, and fantastical creatures peer out from behind scrolling leaves and tendrils. It stretches up three floors beside a spiral staircase that provides access to all floors. The tree incorporates fourteen silk-screened panels and twenty-four broadcasting monitors – a new presentation medium that contrasts with the drawn elements.

The creatures also appear on the walls of the store, inside the fitting rooms, and on pieces of furniture. Several techniques were used to apply these images, including stamping on raw timber. The mixture of hand-printing with digital media is part of the overall graphic direction for the brand. Both techniques allow for a high degree of flexibility. As such, depending on a store's architecture, its location, or its cultural environment, the graphical illustrations can be easily adapted in their theme as well as in their size, quantity, colour, and material.

\03

\04

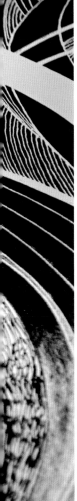

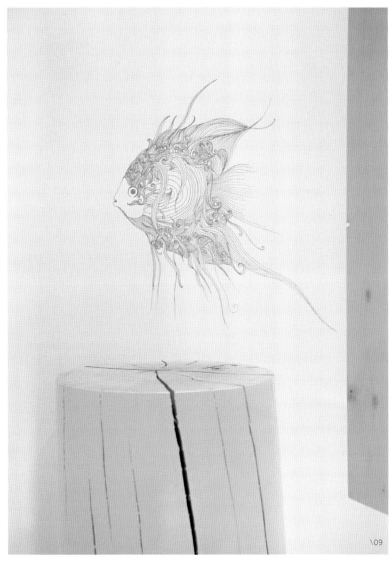

\09

\08

\10

\01, 03, 06: Stamping by hand with specially produced rubber stamps was used as a flexible means of providing brand imagery.

\02: The corporate orange logo was incorporated into the graphics using a linework technique.

\04: The intricate artwork for the "fantasy tree."

\05: Stretching upward beside a spiral staircase, the "fantasy tree" incorporates fourteen silk-screened panels and twenty-four broadcasting monitors.

\07, 08: Details of the silk-screened panels in the "fantasy tree" show the fine scale of the original hand-drawn illustration.

\09: Illustrated animals were given a dream-like quality within the muted context of timber and concrete.

\10: Some of the drawn creatures verge on the grotesque, as if to emphasise the experimentation that BOSS Orange promotes as a quality of the brand.

THE SPAGHETTI HOUSE

HONG KONG, CHINA
design JOEY HO DESIGN
photos COURTESY OF JOEY HO DESIGN

\\\ **Illustrative strands of spaghetti tell a story of joy, humour, and dining pleasures at Hong Kong pasta restaurant The Spaghetti House. Customers are encouraged to share a modern dining experience that communicates aspects of the Italian way of life.**

The Spaghetti House is a Hong Kong-based chain of Italian pasta restaurants that occupies a prominent position in the island's mid-market dining sector. Joey Ho Design was engaged to create an alluring interior for the Tseung Kwan O outlet in Hong Kong's New Territories. The elasticity of spaghetti and the archetypal Italian zest for life became themes that were celebrated with colour and illustration.

Intersecting and gliding around the space are drawings that depict vitality and delight. A continuous bold, spaghetti-like stroke forms a joyful banquet scene on a vibrant red ceiling – a reflection, one would hope, of the dining encounters at the tables below. Black illustrations on white walls portray the beauty of life with a wonderland of animals, birds, trees, and a girl playing a violin.

The physical form of spaghetti strands was translated into wavy mouldings and ceiling edge profiles. In contrast, a black ceiling was covered with a hexagonal matrix of white-painted, die-cut timber elements. The dramatic combinations were designed to communicate a cheerful modern lifestyle. A variety of seating zones – including a main dining "piazza" – encourage relaxation and social experiences.

\05

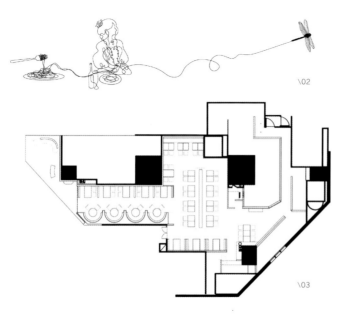

\02

\03

\01: A joyful mood is encouraged by oversized dragonflies, butterflies, horses, birds, trees, curling branches, and a girl with a violin.

\02: A conceptual illustration depicting the lyrical spaghetti strand.

\03: A plan (not to scale) shows the different seating zones – private lounge settings, booths, and a central piazza that can host large gatherings.

\04, 05: Waves of red flow through the space, reflecting light and accommodating drawings.

\06: Tiffany lamps are a staple feature of The Spaghetti House restaurants. Here they received a modern interpretation.

\07, 08: A combination of chair styles lends a relaxed air and complements the illustrated menagerie.

\06

\08

KITINETE

CURITIBA, BRAZIL

conceptualisation MÁRCIA "MAÇÃ" ("APPLE") TOLEDO
coordination GIUSY DE LUCA
artwork BERNARDO BENTO (A.K.A. JEKILL), CLAUDIO RESTON
(A.K.A. HAROLDINHO), FEFE TALAVERA, NOMAD INK (TYLER JOHNSON
AND FLAVIA SANCHES), RENATO FACCINI AND SUNDER RAJ,
RIMON GUIMARÃES, TRISTAN RAULT
photos CARLOS BEZZ

\\\ At Kitinete, there's kitsch in every corner, art
covering every wall, and subversion in the air.
This small, colourful bar in Curitiba, Brazil was
designed to make a night out feel more like a
house party. In Kitinete's cosy, irreverent world,
exaggeration is celebrated, pop nostalgia is
worshipped, and formality is left at the door.

Apolite, conventional modernist interior was not
what Márcia "Maçã" ("Apple") Toledo had in mind for
her bar in Curitiba. Rather, she embarked on a quest for
subversion. She questioned good taste, expectation, and
formality in order to inspire ease, comfort, and interaction.
Kitinete was to be a home-away-from-home for its family of
patrons – a subterranean cathedral of kitsch, both familiar
and fantastical at the same time, where friendships could be
made as easily as a cocktail.

In spatial terms, Kitinete simulates a house. It contains a
kitchen, a petite staircase, and a number of rooms accessed
by narrow doorways. Furthermore, traditional bar furniture
has been usurped by coffee tables, comfortable sofas,
and armchairs, which patrons can move around as they
please. In decorative terms, however, Kitinete more closely
resembles a surreal domestic dreamscape. Old curtain fabric
covers the sofas. Chequered plastic tablecloths line the walls
above the bar. Items usually found on a mantelpiece or in a
toy box are gathered together in menacing tribes.

It is on the walls of Kitinete where subversion is most
heartily embraced. "Apple" invited some of the most
exciting local artists to contribute work. Their expressive,
large-format paintings have turned the entire bar into a
gallery, warping context and scale in an overwhelming
homage to well-intentioned irreverence. In this unique
atmosphere, "Apple" hosts art exhibitions as well as musical
performances, and always welcomes more oddball items for
the Kitinete collection.

\01: Renato Faccini and Sunder Raj
created a homage to the silver age of
comics and artists such as Steve Ditko,
Gene Colan, and Jack Kirby. The final touch
was the romantic song lyrics used in the
dialogue balloons.

\02: A series of caricatures and lettering
by Tyler Johnson and Flavia Sanches of
Nomad Ink represents the group of artists
and managers.

\03: Tristan Rault's collage of words
above the staircase invites contemplation.
Letters are from Fefe Talavera, a São
Paulo graffiti artist.

\04: A vibrant wall of words by designer
and typographer Claudio Reston (a.k.a.
Haroldinho) contains a tongue twister
in Portuguese.

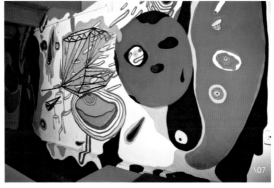

\05, 06: Nomad Ink's mural is full of letterforms from around the world, and creates a 3D space on a 2D surface. To the right, another comic wall by Renato Faccini and Sunder Raj.

\07: Abstraction reigns in the downstairs area, with a playful mural by Rimon Guimarães.

\08: Bernardo Bento's (a.k.a. JEKILL's) interest in Chinese culture manifested in an opium-themed work above the stairs.

ADIDAS ORIGINALS

SINGAPORE
design MOMOROBO
photos KEVIN LIM CHUN HUI

\\\ Seeking a reconnection with traditional cultural values and practices, adidas Originals conceived its "Materials of the World" collection – a fusion of traditional fabrics from around the world with iconic adidas styles. Launching the collection in Singapore was a retail installation that mixed fantasy with reality and took shoppers on an otherworldly visual journey.

Signature traditional fabrics from Peru, Canada, England, Greenland, and Russia (and elsewhere) form the basis of adidas Originals' unique "Materials of the World" collection, which brings a taste of cultural specificity to the sportswear industry. The casual footwear and clothing in the collection is intended to celebrate the originality of the featured fabrics and the stories behind them, as well as the heritage of the adidas brand through a basis on styles from the company's past.

In Singapore, the collection was launched at adidas' flagship store in the Orchard Road shopping zone. Singapore-based art and design collective Momorobo was invited to share its interpretation of the collection with an installation. Using decal stickers and props, Momorobo created artwork that straddled fantasy and reality, and captured the chaotic mixture of impressions – recognition, unfamiliarity, excitement, and fear – that can accompany travel to foreign destinations.

Chaotic collages of contemporary urban and traditional cultural iconography, featuring fantastical creatures and recognisable forms, emblazoned the glazed shopfront as well as internal screens. These candy-coloured jumbles were graphically bound together with threads that reinforced the textile focus of the collection. Opposing the chaos, items from the collection were presented in a gallery-like manner, with museological information cards highlighting the origin of each feature fabric.

\01: A combination of props, decal stickers, and illustrated panels conveys the theme in a light-hearted manner.

\02: Strands of hair weave their way through the candy-coloured explosion of imergery, mimicking thread.

\03: Decal stickers on the shopfront create a semi-permeable visual filter.

\04: A chaotic collage reminds us that despite our differences, we are all part of the same story.

\05: The artwork represents the chaotic mixture of impressions that can accompany journeys to foreign destinations.

\06: A museological-style signage system explains the collection, each of its themes, and the design installation itself.

PLUK

HAARLEM, THE NETHERLANDS
design TJEP.
photos FRANK TJEPKEMA

\\\ Pluk injects an energetic burst into a main
shopping street in Haarlem, The Netherlands.
This health food café and take-away establishment
rejects the idea that healthy means boring. With its
bold colours, installations, and graphics, the small
space is packed with a sense of energy, vitality, and,
most importantly, fun!

Pluk is small, but it's certainly punchy. It offers fresh juices, yogurt shakes, and salads, and allows customers to choose their own salad ingredients. Through its operational system, its identity, and its interior, Pluk promotes the message that healthy food not only makes you feel good, but it can also be great fun.

Design studio Tjep. was engaged to derive an identity, a name, and an interior for Pluk. Enjoying good food is the essence of the Pluk formula, so for Tjep., the emphasis on health was implicit. Pluk contends that if you eat healthy food 99% of the time, it's ok to indulge for the other 1% of the time. Tjep. found a way for the establishment to offer both the 99% and the 1% in a lively juxtaposition.

Tjep. soaked the interior with colour and graphics. Counters containing artificial fruits and vegetables stretch down the narrow space in three colour groups. It took three months for Tjep. to settle on the ideal colours for the glass, but the result is that the plastic fruits and vegetables take on a delicious combination of hues. Photo-based graphics present vegetables and other foods stretching energetically down walls, as though undertaking a gym workout. Bench seating is a fun, watermelon pink colour. Stools – with three legs rather than four and a shape reminiscent of a bicycle seat – appear ready for action.

\03

\04

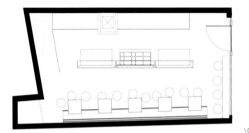

\02

\01, 04: Photographs of foods were stretched to create energetic artwork that reminds customers that healthy eating can be fun and surprising.

\02: A plan (not to scale) shows the use of all available space in the small interior.

\03: The Pluk logo communicates fun and experimentation with its manipulation of rounded letterforms.

\05: Hinting at speed and vitality rather than comfortable lounging, three-legged stools stand out against a dark timber floor. Mirrors at the rear reflect the changing street context and daylight.

\06: The three segments of the counter display plastic fruits and vegetables behind coloured glass. Transparency has been preserved so customers can view the preparation of their items.

\05

\06

BRAD NGATA HAIR DIRECTION (UPTOWN AT IVY)

SYDNEY, AUSTRALIA
design SCOTT WESTON ARCHITECTURE & DESIGN
photos NICHOLAS WATT

\\\ "You're the star, sweetheart!" The service mantra of exclusive Sydney hair salon Brad Ngata Hair Direction couldn't better describe the aura within its second branch – a luxurious French boudoir-inspired interior punctuated with postmodern wit, where silk and crystal coexist theatrically with printed laminate.

A wonderland of bars, restaurants, and shops recently appeared on central Sydney's George Street in the form of a prestigious new complex named Ivy (designed by Woods Bagot with Merivale Group and Hecker Phelan & Guthrie). Brad Ngata Hair Direction was offered an intimate space there, and Ngata – along with co-owner Glenn Chaplin – dreamed up a luscious design direction for their second location. Scott Weston Architecture & Design brought the dream to reality.

Ngata and Chaplin favoured the feel of a sumptuous eighteenth-century French salon, reminiscent of those that royal mistress Madame de Pompadour would have enjoyed – opulent, grand, and theatrical. Scott Weston Architecture & Design embraced the fantasy and devised a luxurious palette of pink silk drapes, plaster ceiling roses, a velvet banquette, and parquetry flooring. Crystal-buttoned, baroque-inspired armchairs were imported, and bevelled mirrors were installed to lend greater visual depth to the modestly sized salon.

The key to the transformation of the space, however, came via the designers' manipulation of one of the most humble modern materials. Selected for its durability, laminate was custom-printed with graphics that mimic classic French panelling. With the traditional carving compressed into a single graphic layer, the postmodern joinery became a glamorous and witty statement on the importance of image and, in the tradition of the pop artists, a comment on our world of mass production and speed. Even so, at this salon, there's still time to smell the roses – with nothing less than a porcelain teacup in hand.

\05

\06

\07

\01: Through the shop window, passersby can picture themselves within the sensuous surrounds via the mirrors at the end of the space.

\02, 03: The comparatively modern reception and circulation areas bear some of the salon's few non-decorated wall panels.

\04: Theatrical pink drapes frame a wall of bevelled mirrors at the end of the boudoir-style space. Clients can view themselves as stars within a stage set.

\05: Custom-printed laminate glamorously wraps the salon's walls and joinery, establishing a theatrical environment.

\06: Crystal-buttoned chairs stand proudly on polished parquetry. A fine attention to detail ensures a theatrical experience for clients.

\07: The mixture of two and three dimensions brings a sense of play to one's experience of this memorable interior.

THE BUTTER FACTORY

SINGAPORE

curation BOBBY LUO
artwork EBOY, JEREMYVILLE, JON BURGERMAN, PESKIMO, RINZEN, TOKIDOKI
photos THE BUTTER FACTORY

\\\ When Singapore nightspot The Butter Factory relocated to a larger venue, its owners were keen to preserve the club's reputation for eccentric partying – an impression that had been aided by its quirky, art-filled interior. The move provided the opportunity to establish fun new interior themes and commission playful scenographic artwork from internationally renowned artists.

After operating for several years in a location beside the Singapore River, nightspot The Butter Factory built up a following significant enough for it to regularly reach capacity. Musically, the club had carved for itself a substantial niche with its focus on hip hop and R&B sounds. Perhaps an equally significant draw was its art-filled interior, which displayed contributions from prominent international pop culture artists and designers and set the context for a fun escape from daily life.

The club's floor area doubled when it relocated to a space beside Singapore's Marina Bay. The Butter Factory's creative director Bobby Luo curated the artwork and design within the new space, commissioning fresh installations and incorporating some of the character artwork from the former venue. In its past and present guises, the club has incorporated contributions from more than 200 artists. The new space is divided into two large rooms, within which artwork and props communicate fun themes and establish zones of various scales.

The main room (titled "Bump") depicts residential spaces with imagery created by British artist duo Peskimo. The dance floor portrays a backyard swimming pool with a rippling interactive projected floor and tiled drinks tables (to Luo's design) from which life buoys hang. Also featured within the "House of Peskimo" are a faux fireplace, a portrait wall, and a trophy cabinet (filled with toys designed by Peskimo). The second room (titled "Fash") is themed "Discopolis" and contains interpretations of cities from artists and designers including Rinzen, Jeremyville, eBoy, Jon Burgerman, and Tokidoki.

\02

\04

\05

\06

\07

\01: Graphic walls by Australian design and art collective Rinzen portray urban icons and abstract characters.

\02: Artwork brings an intimate scale to a large space.

\03: Jeremyville, an artist based in both New York and Sydney, created this large-format urban mural for the "Discopolis" room.

\04: A fanciful, pixellated London-scape by eBoy – a trio of designers based in Berlin and Vancouver – wraps around a corner in the "Discopolis" room.

\05: British duo Peskimo created domestic-themed artworks for the "House of Peskimo" room, including this faux fireplace and portrait wall.

\06: Peskimo's mantelpiece and window setting depicts a strange backyard scene and an elaborate bonsai plant.

\07: Within the "House of Peskimo," a swimming pool setting demarcates the dance floor. Character artworks from the previous venue were also installed (such as the tofu characters by KAME & L.N.K.).

ROC MONDRIAAN

THE HAGUE, THE NETHERLANDS

graphic design EELCO VAN DEN BERG
art direction BLUE LEMON
photos COURTESY OF EELCO VAN DEN BERG

\\\ ROC Mondriaan, a vocational training institution in The Hague, engaged illustrator Eelco van den Berg to create a series of large-scale graphic works that would appear throughout its premises. His colourful artwork brings attention to the varied content of ROC Mondriaan's courses, and provides contemporary visualisations that fill the school with energy.

ROC Mondriaan is one of a number of ROC schools in The Netherlands that offers vocational training, general education, and job-related courses for youth and adults. With the aim of enhancing the interior character of the ROC Mondriaan building, art director Blue Lemon asked illustrator Eelco van den Berg to implement a series of large-scale wallpaper and window foil prints in corridors, a multimedia library, and a canteen.

The artwork was to correspond to the existing interior colours and bring a sense of intimacy to large areas. Primarily, however, van den Berg was asked to communicate the function of each space, and thus derive a visual expression of specific programs and of study in general. Recalling his own experiences of dull school environments, he worked to create lively imagery and pique the interest of students.

van den Berg drew many of the images by hand before manipulating them digitally. He mixed subject-specific imagery with a variety of other illustrative elements that would provide a link between different spaces. He dynamically layered images of various scales and assembled them in swathes that draw the eye from one end of a wall plane to the other. The active, affirming imagery offers reinforcement to students of the roles they will soon play in the workplace, and the possibilities open to them.

\03

\04

\02

\01: In the multimedia library, a wallpaper stretches thirty metres in length and five metres in height. The exciting possibilities enabled by study and dedication are reinforced with iconic imagery.

\02: In the canteen, a mixture of wallpapers and window foils depict foods and drinks.

\03: The scale of the imagery suits the vastness of the multimedia library and allows for the wall to be read from a distance.

\04: The programs taught on each floor are depicted on wallpaper. The fashion design and hairdressing programs are illustrated in the third floor corridor.

\05: Security and foreign languages are taught on the first floor. The layering of imagery and the depiction of active characters bring dynamism and energy to the corridor.

\06: Programs in economy and nursing are taught on the second floor. The use of non-iconic character faces helps students to imagine themselves in the work context.

\05

\06

ECLIPSE

MELBOURNE, AUSTRALIA
design ZWEI INTERIORS ARCHITECTURE
graphics/illustrations SALMON DESIGN
photos UTE WEGMANN

\\\ The Eclipse café is located within a heritage-listed building that forms part of a prestigious central Melbourne hotel. Despite its exclusive and historic surrounds, the café resonates with a modest and gritty tone that expresses the buzz of contemporary life in the space.

Tucked into the rear of central Melbourne's InterContinental (Rialto) Hotel, Eclipse attracts a steady stream of city workers and coffee connoisseurs through its discreet Flinders Lane entrance. The café sits within a heritage-listed brick building that was constructed in 1891 in the Queen Anne style. Eclipse was designed in a manner that weaves the café fitout with the heritage shell of the space.

Zwei Interiors Architecture stripped back the shell to reveal raw brickwork, and inserted new surfaces, fixtures, and furniture with a modest approach. Texture, pattern, and lighting effects characterise the space. Plywood, with its distinct grain patterns, was applied to walls, ceiling, and tabletops as a complement to the textured brick walls. Like the mouldings and pillars of the building's façade, stripes of colourful mosaic tiles were applied rhythmically to walls. They feature small pigeonhole displays for coffee paraphernalia. The dramatic lighting design within the space creates bright and dark areas – a clever play on the café's name.

Collaborating studio Salmon Design developed artwork that brings another layer of texture to the interior – a narrative of the lived history of the space. Illustrations engraved onto the plywood wall panels depict scenes of present-day workers making coffee and roasting coffee beans. The hand-drawn style reinforces Zwei's modest approach to the interior design, and resonates with a sense of immediacy befitting a busy café.

\01: Illuminated by a series of colourful pendants, the preparation and serving area dominates the interior. The raw brick walls are dramatised by fittings that cast light both upward and downward.

\02: Flatness meets depth in the combination of mosaic tiles, pigeonhole displays, and perspectival drawings.

\03: A plywood ceiling brings definition to the service counter.

\04: A dark atmosphere pervades areas of the interior not captured by the feature and accent lighting. The illustrations were engraved onto the plywood panels.

\02

\03

\04

MOTIF

SAN JOSE, USA
design MR IMPORTANT
photos FARRAH KARAPETIAN

\\\ In the two-level, dual-function establishment Motif, materials have been put to work in the creation of a glamorous atmosphere that works both during the day and at night. This San Jose restaurant and nightclub explores and experiments with several unusual materials, as well as coloured light, to create a vibrant mixture that keeps its guests entertained.

Designer Mr Important approached the choreography of this large two-level space in gritty San Jose by mixing things up. The lower level functions as a double-height restaurant – a space for chilled-out afternoons and refined dinners – and the upper level accommodates a late-night dance club. When the club heats up, though, the restaurant morphs into a colour-soaked lounge. Mr Important swathed the interior with unusual materials and varied design references, as well as coloured light, to bring unity to the establishment.

Hundreds of feet of black and silver chain have been hand-worked into a number of bold floral screens – super-scaled installations (stretching up two storeys) to a design by Amy Butler. Partially transparent and interactive, the screens envelope spaces without suffocating them. Overhead, an installation of seven thousand pieces of black glass form two huge leaf shapes. They were created by installation and chandelier designer Eva Menz, and they hover gracefully over the downstairs restaurant like passing clouds.

The fine-grained materiality of the restaurant space gives way to a more fluid, light-doused environment as the night wears on. Colour-changing LEDs transform the monochrome environment into a heady polychromatic lounge and club experience. Stretched glossy polymer film provides a futuristic, undulating ceiling of reflected colour and pattern above the DJ area, and pop-inspired graphics featuring baroque-style chairs hark back to past centuries to reinforce the mixture of aesthetics.

\01: Many lengths of black and silver chain have been installed to create a permeable, super-scaled floral screen that stretches up the full height of the double-volume space.

\02: Later in the evenings, when the upstairs dance club comes alive, coloured light washes the restaurant and it functions as a lounge. Mezzanine seating overhangs the restaurant on two sides.

\03: A wave of suspended black glass pieces flows over the restaurant like a cloud or a wave.

\04: Furniture in the mezzanine VIP seating area continues the semi-transparent aesthetic.

\05: The floral chain screens become the medium for an elaborate display of changing coloured light.

\06: Graphics in the dance club add another aesthetic to the rich mixture.

LINDEN APOTHEKE

LUDWIGSBURG, GERMANY

design IPPOLITO FLEITZ GROUP – IDENTITY ARCHITECTS
artwork MONICA TRENKLER
photos ZOOEY BRAUN

\\\ Changing the nature of its business from drugs to natural products required Linden Apotheke, an old and established German pharmacy, to significantly rebrand. The new retail interior suggests the company's professionalism and precision, but also the pleasure of a cup of herbal tea.

LINDEN APOTHEKE
LUDWIGSBURG

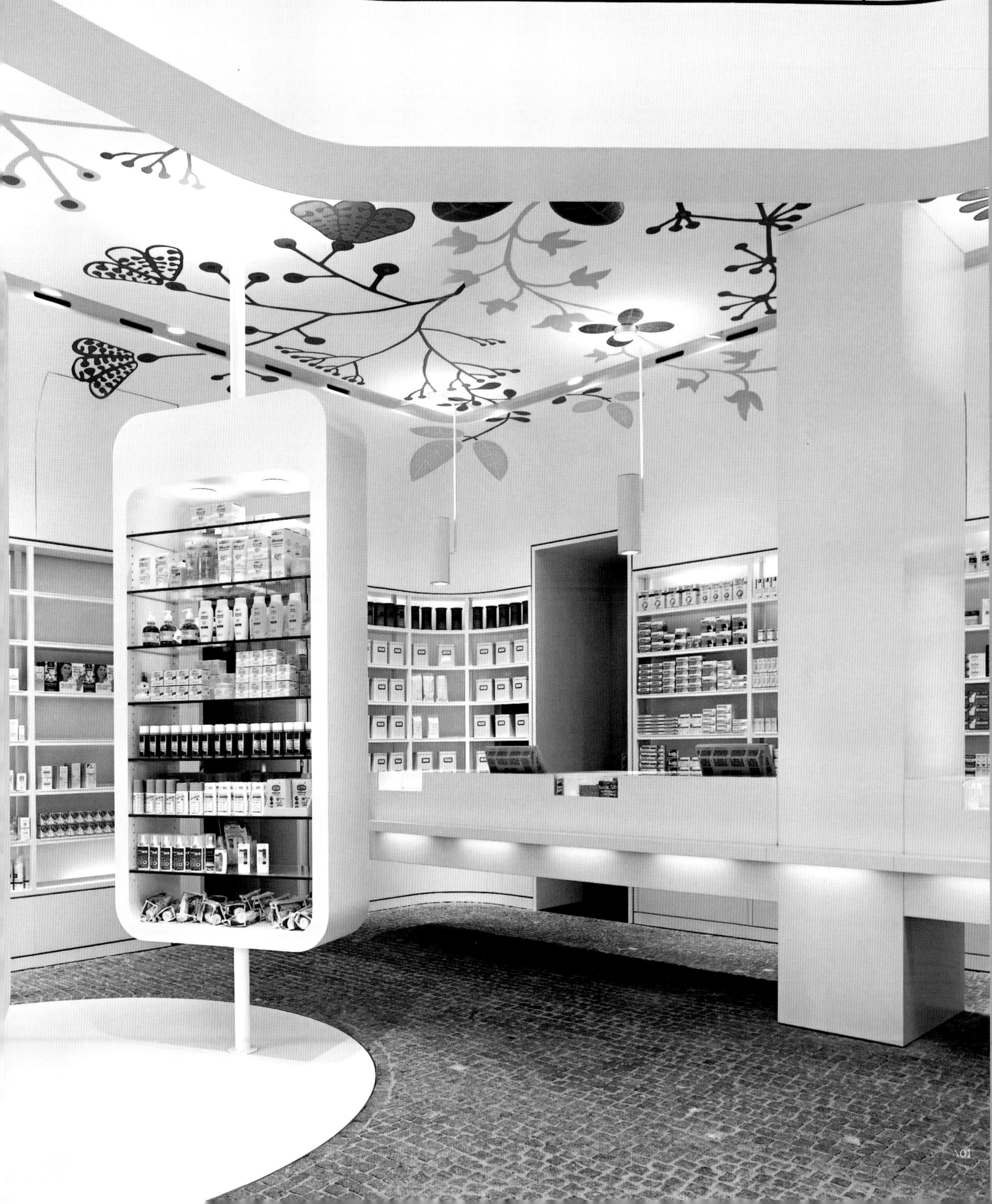

\01

The owners of Linden Apotheke boldly responded to ever-greater competition in the pharmacy market by turning to naturopathic products and natural cosmetics. A significant didactical effort was required to communicate this fundamental change. Ippolito Fleitz Group was engaged to create an interior and corporate identity that would reflect the new natural product range and leave a lasting mental image.

The shop space was reorganised to create a compact, high-ceilinged room that can be easily understood from the striking entrance. The latter is cut from a curving white wall that fluidly wraps around the shop's corners – also curving up to meet the ceiling. Contributing further to the aesthetic of sleek computer-generated forms, a white sales counter cantilevers stoically from a column, and rounded, rotatable merchandise stands hover over a white disc. The impression is one of clarity and modernity.

Counteracting this is a granite cobblestone floor – a clear reference to a time prior to the widespread use of chemical science in medicine. The expansive ceiling fresco, conceived with textile designer Monica Trenkler, depicts eleven medicinal herbs in a contemporary style. Appearing to grow past a recessed lighting track, from ceiling to walls, the fresco is memorable and optimistic – a strong visual that also adorns corporate documents and packaging.

\03

\04

\01: Space age curves and cobblestones collide beneath a herbal fresco. Natural products are contained within pristine white cabinetry.

\02: Fitted with concealed lighting for additional emphasis, the sales counter cantilevers impressively from a column in a statement of contemporary can-do.

\03: Set well into the shop space, the entrance steps deposit customers directly into the medley of motifs.

\04: Three rotatable merchandise stands are underscored by a disc of clinical white epoxy resin on the floor.

\05: The medicinal herb ceiling fresco is a modern interpretation of a traditional subject and has become the new emblem of the pharmacy.

BAUER

STOCKHOLM, SWEDEN
design DIZEL&SATE
photos COURTESY OF DIZEL&SATE

\\\ An embrace of intriguing mixtures seems an appropriate way to approach the design of a tapas restaurant. Bauer's variety of small snacks is served in an interior that references German design and culture, Walt Disney, and the realm of nightlife. What's more, Bauer is located on an ever-changing street in Stockholm. Confused? Don't be.

Swedish design studio Dizel&Sate is becoming known for not wanting to be known for anything in particular. The studio seeks the unexpected with its interior and graphic work, and Bauer was no exception to this rule. The restaurant is located in Stockholm's Södermalm district, on Götgatan – a street heavily trafficked by pedestrians. Dizel&Sate's aim was to capture the contrasts of Götgatan and the neighbourhood, which is constantly undergoing change.

Bauer's guests find themselves face-to-face with a gang of cartoon-like figures who glare cutely from walls and lampshades. Beneath them, however, dining and lounging settings sit nonchalantly in hues of black and white. The designers took inspiration from the 1920s Bauhaus style (which is evident in elements such as the steel-framed furniture and spherical pendant lights), but also from Berlin's new gallery and bar culture, with its mixture of grittiness and refinement.

But what inspired the playful characters? The aim was to represent different types of pleasures and senses – thoughts, visions, flavours, dreams, the joys of nightlife, and so on. A smirking pink mouse, a one-eyed bear, a hypnotised owl, and a pair of staring eyes are among the unruly gang of characters that calls Walt Disney to mind – albeit in a corrupted fashion. What message could one possible take from Bauer? Surely: don't take life too seriously.

\03

\04

\01: Chipboard clashes deliberately with cartoon-style graphics, an ornate cornice, and reductive furniture.

\02: A variety of symbols and shapes compose a wallpaper pattern that shifts in resonance from machines to cartoons.

\03: A photographic collage brings glimpses of reality to the dining area.

\04: Dizel&Sate's Slobodan Zivic and Thomas Berger at Bauer.

\05: Cute animated figures in the lounge area were designed to indicate different senses and types of pleasures.

FILINI

LIVERPOOL, UK
design BURNEVERYTHING and R2 ARCHITECTURE
photos CRAIG MAGEE

\\\ Situated within Liverpool's Radisson Hotel, Italian restaurant Filini at once comforts guests with the reassurance of the familiar, and challenges them with contemporary explorations and reinterpretations. Leather, chandeliers, filigree screens, and graphic walls combine to impart an Italian character that reaffirms traditions and celebrates the new.

Design studio Burneverything collaborated with R2 Architecture to redesign Filini. While a captivating reinvention of the space was the objective, it was equally vital that the establishment retain its appeal to the varied people who form the hotel's population at any time. Furthermore, it was necessary for the design of Filini to be suitable to two divergent functions – a restaurant for fine evening dining (offering an intimate experience), and a breakfast room (offering an open, bright experience).

The design team took an approach that combined classic Italian materials, motifs, and colours with contemporary production techniques and aesthetics. A classic Italian character was sought with a rich, comforting treatment of deep red paint (on both walls and ceiling), plush red curtains, vintage red leather, and timber. Elaborate chandeliers bring a glamorous impression to one end of the restaurant, while black pendants – elegantly utilitarian in shape – are stylistically suitable to both morning and evening dining.

In the morning, the interior is dappled with light shining through filigree screens, which create partial enclosure and allow glimpses of Liverpool's River Mersey. Reinterpreting an ancient craft, the designers created the teak-veneered screens with a laser cutting technique. The cut-out shapes were gleaned from a drawing created for wallpaper that wraps a dining niche – a contemporary grotto of sorts. Owls, eagles (a traditional motif used in heraldry), architecture, leaves, and flowers are collaged to offer a fresh perspective of some classic Italian motifs.

\01: A dining niche is a contemporary grotto of sorts – bright and white rather than dim and damp. Graphic wallpaper and angular chairs create a contemporary aesthetic that co-exists with traditional marble.

\02: The filigree screens provide partial enclosure to the restaurant, and offer glimpses of the River Mersey. The rich colours and materials are dappled when sunlight shines directly through the screens.

\03: The traditional craft of filigree was reinterpreted with laser-cut plywood and teak veneer.

\04, 05: Classic Italian motifs were collaged to create the wallpaper graphic that is at once romantic and modern.

ABSTRACT

OHWOW BOOK CLUB

NEW YORK, USA
design RAFAEL DE CÁRDENAS (ARCHITECTURE AT LARGE)
photos FLOTO + WARNER

\\\ **OHWOW Book Club doesn't look like your average bookshop. It should come as little surprise, therefore, that this subterranean New York space stocks titles that you're unlikely to find on Main Street. The artist-produced books and objects of creative collective OHWOW find an ideal setting in this discreet and intentionally disorienting chamber.**

Tucked away beneath a historic brownstone-clad building on Waverly Place in Greenwich Village is a tiny space with an intention that is considerably larger. OHWOW is a creative collective based in Miami and led by Aaron Bondaroff and Al Moran. The duo draws people from the worlds of art, fashion, music, design, and publishing into a community where creative endeavours straddle different media. Their aim is to dissolve established ideas and expectations about creative practice – to build what they call "a heterotopic arena for cultural projects."

For OHWOW Book Club, Bondaroff and Moran bestowed the task of translating this vision into a tangible retail space upon their architect-friend Rafael de Cárdenas. To represent the atypical and the displaced, de Cárdenas set out to give the 150-square-foot (14-square-metre) space a sense of disorientation and chaos.

He drew on a variety of motifs, including the stepping patterns commonly found in Navajo blankets, and the aesthetic of classic black-and-white pre-war New York City bathrooms. The rectilinear geometry established by the tiling and stepped shelving is reinforced by an uncompromising bank of overhead fluorescent lights. It is challenged, however, by the layered patterns of brushstrokes and angular shapes (of reflective Mylar polyester film) on the walls. The shelves appear to be both stacked and floating, and while feelings of disorientation set in, bulb lights focus the attention on OHWOW's unique collection of cultural fragments.

\01: The stepped shelving seems to hover between the ceiling and floor planes. Negative space behind the shelves lends the floating sensation.

\02: External stairs lead to the sharply lit underground space and the surprise of a thoroughly atypical bookstore.

\03, 04: With its combination of motifs, styles, colours, and materials, the interior reflects the creative mash-up aspired to by the founders of OHWOW.

SOS FLAGSHIP STORE

STOCKHOLM, SWEDEN

design GUISE
photos JESPER LINDSTRÖM

\\\ The designers of skiwear brand SOS – Sportswear of Sweden – are also skiers, and their garments are known for practical, modest shapes and bold colours that stand out in the monochromatic snow landscape. The brand's flagship store in Stockholm was designed to resemble the layered, snow-laden, and sloping conditions in which SOS apparel is worn.

Skiing involves and demands a total immersion of the body, mind, and senses in the environment. Aiming to communicate a sense of that immersion, Swedish studio Guise designed the SOS Flagship Store as a slope-filled environment that, like a natural landscape, allows for the perception of beauty and encourages feelings of awe.

Guise created a layered experience of the shop space by manipulating one's perception of mass and distance. Curving white walls – solid and uncompromising in appearance – carve up the space and demarcate a fitting area to one side. They bestow a strong physical presence and direct customer movement into the centre of the store. Around the perimeter, however, there appears to be a dissolving boundary – a multi-layered forest of trunks and branches. Two layers of CNC-cut panels stand in front of a white perimeter wall, creating the illusion of snowy alpine timbers.

While SOS clothing is brightly coloured, it is modest and clean in shape – designed primarily with functional considerations. Similarly, the display furniture designed by Guise has a simple square shape in plan. However, it incorporates steep display surfaces to resemble the oblique forms of mountains. The rubber display surfaces were generally given the maximum possible steepness without the possibility of the garments sliding off. Steel plates beneath the rubber on particularly steep surfaces enable the clothing to be pinned down using magnets. High-gloss finishes add to the perception of icy conditions, piquing one's awareness of the need for care and the proper equipment on the slopes.

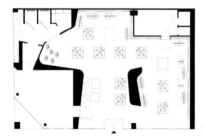

\02

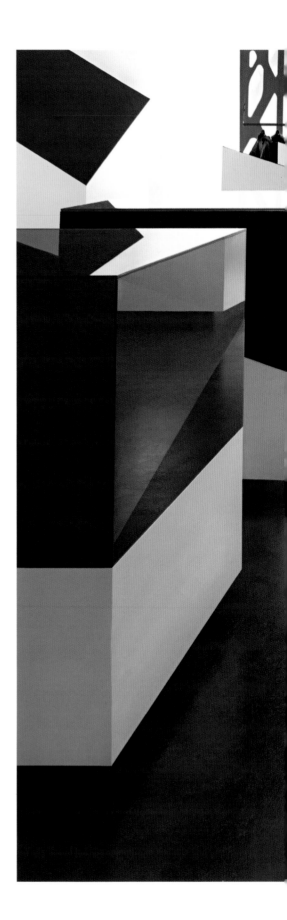

\01: The store was restricted to a palette of white and black to allow the colourful SOS garments to stand out (as they do in the snow).

\02: A plan of the store (not to scale).

\03: High-gloss finishes impart an icy appearance and reflect light around the space.

\04: The sloping display furniture was designed to resemble the mountainous conditions familiar to skiers.

\05: Additional cavernous display spaces were built into the display furniture.

\06: Delicately cut panels are layered at the store's perimeter to resemble a snow-laden forest receding into the distance.

PHARMACY AT LA PUEBLA 15

PALENCIA, SPAIN
design BUJ+COLÓN ARQUITECTOS
photos LUIS DÍAZ DÍAZ

\\\ In the northern Spanish city of Palencia is a pharmacy that serves as both an operational retail outlet and an urban installation. Inviting the gaze of passersby through its filter-like perimeter, Pharmacy at La Puebla 15 is an architectural representation of reality, illusion, and the boundary between them.

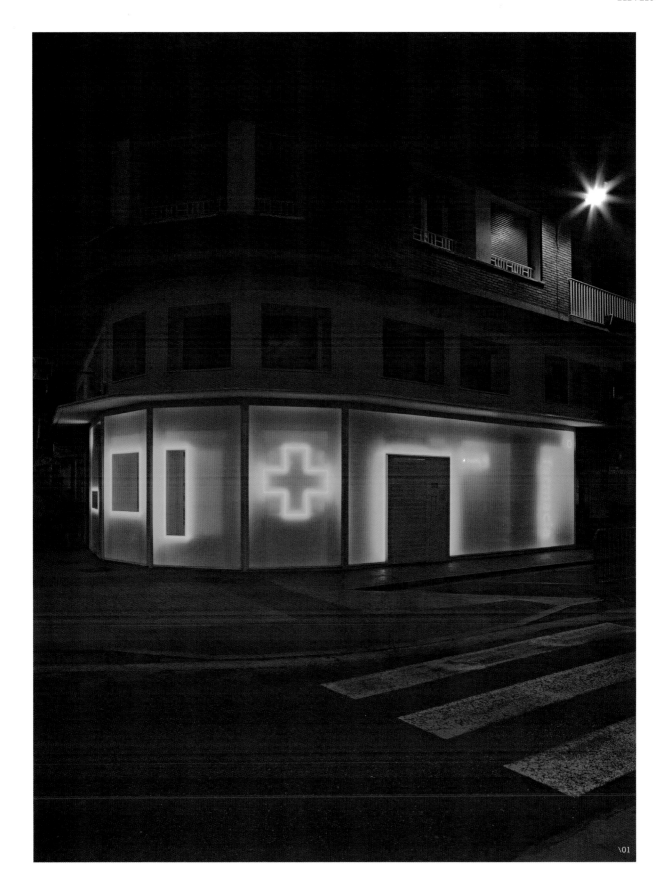

Multiple associations can be assigned to the term "pharmacy." Two dimensions of the term – the conscious and the unconscious – were the focus of Buj+Colón Arquitectos when they designed Pharmacy at La Puebla 15. Regarding illusion as the boundary between the conscious and unconscious experience of pharmacology, the architects considered how they might represent the boundary between reality and illusion in architectural terms.

The spatial distinction between reality and illusion was imagined as a plane of no thickness – a boundary of light. The boundary of the pharmacy – the expansive glazing that wraps around the street corner – was transformed into a glowing plane punctuated by shapes and symbols of light. Though only the shapes glow, it appears that the entire facade is lit as the translucent glazing material partially reflects the green illumination. The illusion of a plane of light lends the pharmacy a surreal air at night.

The architects further explored the idea of the boundary by diverging from the traditional pharmacy arrangment where customers are separated from the products by a sales counter. Instead, the medication is placed on the same plane as the customer. The customer's opportunity to interact more readily with the products begins at the footpath, where glimpses of the interior can be captured through the light-rimmed shapes. These transparent-glazed voids act as filters. A second filter takes the form of internal display shelving that separates public and private areas within the pharmacy. Light shines through the shelves and one perceives a depth of space.

\02

\03

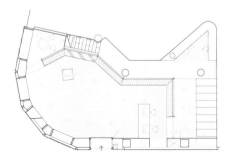

\04

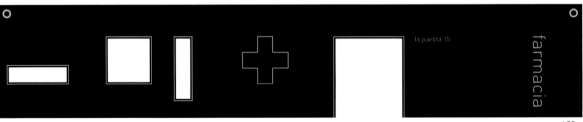

\05

\06

\07

\08

\09

\10

\01: Shapes and symbols appear as ephemeral traces – as abstract elements in the dark.

\02: Voids rimmed by green light punctuate the perimeter boundary and allow glimpses of the interior.

\03, 06: At night, the green light washes over the translucent glazing, creating the illusion of an illuminated plane.

\04: A layout plan (not to scale).

\05: A drawing of the façade concept (not to scale).

\07: The wrapping of the façade around the street corner creates instances where the illusory boundary can be viewed within itself.

\08: Reflective glass shelving creates the perception of additional depth.

\09: The green-washed perimeter viewed from within the pharmacy.

\10: Customers are not segregated from the products as they are in traditional pharmacies.

ARA PIZZA

SANT QUIRZE DEL VALLÈS, SPAIN

design PABLO TÉLLEZ
photos JUAN VENTURA

\\\ The (often) communal experience of eating a pizza is respected and celebrated at Ara Pizza, located just outside Barcelona. The dining space within this fast food restaurant is unified by a sculptural, segmented ceiling, which offers a variable experience of the interior depending on where one positions their moveable table.

When he embarked on the design of Ara Pizza, Pablo Téllez was determined for the restaurant to distance itself from the loud and garish atmospheres he had experienced in many fast food outlets. His graceful interior scheme of muted abstract triangles, nestling tables, and easygoing artwork has resulted in a sophisticated and airy space where both food and design can be enjoyed. It is also a space where customers are granted the opportunity to arrange the furniture to their liking.

Ara Pizza occupies a former blacksmith's workshop in the Spanish town of Sant Quirze del Vallès, which is situated thirty minutes from Barcelona's city centre. Téllez divided the space into two main areas – one serving takeaway customers and fulfilling home delivery orders, and the other dedicated to dine-in customers. The latter is the dominant area. The space had the luxury of an extremely high ceiling, which Téllez accentuated with a series of prism-shaped spaces at different heights. Like an overhead landscape, the ceiling installation produces a variety of light effects.

The custom-designed tables (constructed with a CNC-milled wood fibre board) were the result of a study of how people tend to use such dining spaces. The tables can be nested together to accommodate various group sizes. Artwork was hand-drawn in a casual style to distance the establishment yet further from the loud graphics common to many fast food chains. Animals are depicted interacting with various restaurant products in a humorous manner.

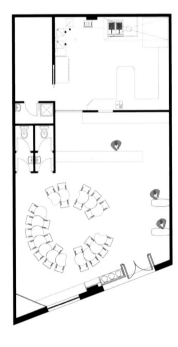

\03

\04

\05

\06

\07

\08

\09

\01: Like a segmented pizza, the ceiling installation is a composition of triangles. The effect is replicated on the walls with various muted paint tones.

\02: A subtle colouration of the façade, along with hand-drawn artwork, identifies the restaurant.

\03: A plan drawing (not to scale) shows how the tables can be arranged in a circular format.

\04, 05, 06: Lightweight chairs and tables were specified in the same range of muted colours.

\07: One's sense of flatness and depth is challenged by the abstract configuration of colour and plane.

\08, 09: The restaurant's artwork features animals humorously interacting with food items.

\10: Signage for the men's and women's conveniences also takes the casual illustrative style. The serving and preparation area is distinguished with a warm orange shade.

HOW LONG IS A PIECE OF STRING?

MELBOURNE, AUSTRALIA
design GLOSS CREATIVE
photos MARCEL AUCAR

\\\ **Visual merchandising or public art? Gloss Creative's installation at the entrance of a Melbourne fashion store embodies brand qualities and grabs attention while also offering an interactive experience to passersby. This colourful work of string art demonstrates the possibilities of creative expression in the storefront domain.**

The design of storefront installations requires a finely tuned process of balance between many considerations – visual impact, the expression of brand, an immediacy of comprehension, the ignition of curiosity, and simplicity of construction. Critically, an installation must be powerful enough to generate a sense of connection in passersby. Gloss Creative's interactive installation at the entrance to central Melbourne's Sportsgirl fashion store demonstrates the possibilities of a retail installation that veers towards public art.

Sportsgirl is an Australian fashion brand for young women that markets an image of fun, playfulness, and quirkiness. In this spirit, the designers at Gloss Creative drew inspiration from cheerful summer days and the endless hours they spent creating craft as children. They devised a vibrant, multi-dimensional work of string art that occupies the wide, open frontage of Sportsgirl's Centerpoint Mall store on Bourke Street.

How Long is a Piece of String? incorporates fluorescent cord, black-painted angular metal frames, and digital printing. Its permeability encourages customers to look through and beyond to the store interior. The layered configuration of this robust installation also entices navigation around it for the full appreciation of its angles and curves. The installation's title is a British and Australian phrase that serves as an answer to a question that cannot be answered with a quantified amount – for example, "How long will it take?" In the context of Sportsgirl's playful approach to fashion and personal identity, it offers a fitting play of words.

\01: The installation allowed the potential customer to grasp enticing glimpses of the store interior.

\02: One's navigation around the installation revealed its three-dimensionality.

\03: The fluorescent cord was wound around screws attached at regular intervals to the frames.

\04: The installation made a strong singular design statement that could be quickly appreciated.

\05: Printed wall film accurately depicted the physical string and cast one's perception of form and dimension into disarray.

how long is a piece of string?

\04

how long is a piece of string?

\05

SVARTENSGATAN 7

STOCKHOLM, SWEDEN
design DIZEL&SATE
photos FREDRIK SWEGER and DIZEL&SATE

\\\ Stockholm salon Svartensgatan 7 required
a fresh direction for its interior and collateral
materials. The salon was redefined with a
futuristic theme inspired by both its address
and our increasingly abstract urban and digital
existence. Svartensgatan 7 is electrified, bright,
and full of movement, with the possibility of chaos
looming somewhere on the horizon.

Svartensgatan 7 is named after the number at which it resides on Södermalm's Svartensgatan street. The figure "7" was to become a prominent influence upon the work of Dizel&Sate, who redesigned the salon's interior and its graphic profile. The influence of "7" is first encountered in the salon's street signage – an installation of fluorescent tubes within a transparent acrylic box that is bolted resolutely to a historic stone-faced wall. The futuristic fluorescent "7" became the salon's new logo, as well as a key generator of the interior concept.

The salon occupies a dark space within an eighteenth-century building, and required a careful treatment of illumination, spatial division, and materiality in order to make the best use of the light generated within. Glass screens, ceiling light panels, and large mirrors allow for the transmission of light around and between areas. A cluster of lights with tangled cords hangs with apparent randomness, perhaps suggesting that chaos is a perpetual possibility in an increasingly urbanised and digitised world.

On wallpapers and glass films, urban scenes and images of people are distorted and mixed with typography. The angles cast by the figure "7" inspired the angularity apparent throughout the space, including the sloping sides of the reception counters. Within this futuristic, abstracted context, a ceramic Virgin Mary prays within a glass cabinet – an icon of serenity illuminated by a tangle of electricity.

\02

\03

abcdefghijklmnopqrstuvxyzåäö
ABCDEFGHIJKLMNOPQRSTUVXYZÅÄÖ
1234567890 $%&(‚‚:;‘’“”!?)

\04

\01: A tangle of lights shines on a cluster of box seats and display cases, illuminating a praying Virgin Mary ceramic statue. Timber tones contrast with abstract black and white.

\02: A fluorescent "7" makes distinctive street signage and establishes the futuristic, electric theme.

\03, 04: The salon's bags, font, and business cards are appropriately themed.

\05: Oblique angles, inspired by the number seven, appear repeatedly throughout the space – on the sloping sides of the lacquered MDF reception counters, on the edge of a glass screen, and in wallpaper graphics.

\06: A ceiling light panel illuminates a dark hallway. A vivid green curtain contrasts with the subtle colour palette of black, white, grey, and timber tones.

\07: Urban scenes, images of people, and typography were collaged and manipulated to create internal wallpaper graphics.

\08: Transparent and reflective materials maximise light within the dark space, which has limited access to natural light. The futuristic theme resonates within a shampooing area.

FRANZESCO

LINZ, AUSTRIA
design X ARCHITEKTEN
photos RUPERT ASANGER

\\\ In the competitive and fast-paced takeaway food industry, a strong and easily understood brand identity is crucial for the capture of a steady stream of customers. Austrian pizzeria Franzesco attracts takeaway and dine-in customers with a bold and bright interior that plays on the shape of pizza boxes and the colours of the Italian flag.

\01

\02

Franzesco enjoys a high-visibility location on a busy retail street near the Linz railway station. With a tram stop right outside, the restaurant's owners recognised the need to grab attention within the streetscape and catch the eye of those approaching at speed. They wished to develop a bold corporate identity that could also be applied to future Franzesco outlets. Austrian architecture firm x architekten developed an abstract geometric theme that has been applied to multiple elements within the small interior.

A bright, open, airy, and unambiguous room identity was established with a pattern of red and green squares on a white background. The colours of the Italian flag are immediately recognisable. The architects developed the forty-centimetre-square pixels as a complement to the circular shape of pizzas, and to reflect the shape of pizza boxes. Floor, walls, ceiling, lighting, furniture, signage, and display cases have all been designed in accordance with the squared aesthetic. The abstract nature of the theme will allow for variations on its expression in future outlets with no loss of the sense of branding.

The coloured squares also appear on the restaurant's façade, communicating a bold presence to the street and establishing the square theme as an integral part of Frazesco's corporate identity. Franzesco is particularly dominant in its streetscape at night, when the bright interior glows.

\04

\05

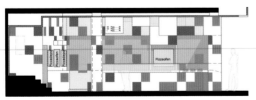

\03

\06

\07

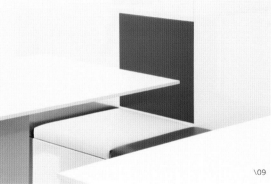

\09

\10

\08

\11

\01: With its red, white, and green palette, Franzesco is resolutely Italian. The square theme was also applied to furniture, signage, and lighting.

\02: Colour is most solidly expressed at the entrance. The coloured squares are also expressed on the restaurant's front façade.

\03: A sectional elevation drawing (not to scale) showing the main counter.

\04: With a potential stream of customers exiting trams right outside, the interior was designed for visual impact in its street context.

\05: A concept illustration by x architekten is suggestive of lightness, layering, and movement. The stripes of the Italian flag gradually dissolve into squares.

\06: A street front display case serves takeaway customers with immediacy.

\07: Substantial unhindered glazing aids in the attraction of customers.

\08: The size and style of menu signage has been controlled to complement the interior.

\09, 10, 11: Linoleum flooring, upholstery fabric, and wall cladding each express the colourful theme.

MAYGREEN

HAMBURG, GERMANY
design KINZO
photos CHRIS MIDDLETON (UNLESS OTHERWISE STATED)

\\\ With its high-tech style, the interior of German eco fashion store MAYGREEN challenges some common conceptions about how to represent environmental awareness through interior design. Though it favours the technical over the raw or roughly hewn, MAYGREEN references natural environments – albeit in an abstract manner.

\01

\02

Eco-friendly, fair-trade fashion store MAYGREEN was established in Hamburg's Ottensen neighbourhood to offer sustainable fashion with a high design value. Intending to diverge from the mainstream of fashion, the store's owners also turned away from common representations of "green" design for their store interior. They engaged Berlin-based studio KINZO – known for a futuristic design style – to infuse the store with a forward-looking flavour.

KINZO established a muted backdrop for the clothing, and installed perimeter rails to accommodate most of the collection. Selected pieces are displayed on low, polygonal platforms that seem to float on the dark oak floor like icebergs. It is possible to view the platforms as a pertinent reminder of a changing climate. On the rear wall is the image of a grasshopper composed of shades of green light. The light shines through a pattern of small holes (developed from a greyscale image) that were laser-cut into the sheet metal wall cladding.

The influence of technology on the store's design is most prevalent in the overhead lighting installation, which lures customers from the entrance into the centre of the space. The arrangement of green cables and low-energy lights resembles the graphic patterns on circuit boards and computer chips. Every cable is covered with green nylon mesh and ends at a pendant or ceiling-mounted light. The latter were designed by KINZO and specially manufactured for MAYGREEN by German lighting specialist idee.design.licht.

\03

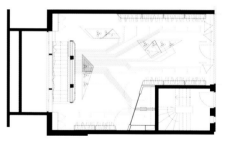

\04

\06

\07

\08

\01, 02: A light installation at the rear
wall depicts a grasshopper, and offers an
abstract representation of nature.

\03, 06: An overhead network of cables
and lights was designed to resemble the
patterns on computer chips. Its branches
illuminate the various display areas and
lure customers to the centre of the space.

\04: A combined floor and lighting plan
(not to scale).

\05: The shard-like polygonal display
platforms seem to float on the floor
like icebergs.

\07, 08: Each of the specially designed,
low-energy ceiling-mounted lights
(manufactured by idee.design.licht)
incorporates a UV block to prevent the
bleaching of textiles. Photos by idee.
design.licht.

SWATCH INSTANT II

BERLIN, GERMANY

design FUENTEYFUENTE, JACQUES ET BRIGITTE, PIXELPUNK
photos FUENTEYFUENTE, JACQUES ET BRIGITTE, PIXELPUNK

\\\ The re-design of the Swatch Instant store in Berlin was to be completed in a veritable instant – within just three days. A team of three design practices shaped a playful, perspective-bending reinterpretation, taking into account the formal complexity of the store's existing architecture.

\01

\02

\03

\04

Launched in 2005, the Swatch Instant stores are among the first ever pop-up stores. They are based on the use of modular furniture designed by Thilo Fuente – an approach that allows a new store interior to be designed and installed extremely quickly. Instant stores have appeared in eleven different European cities. Every store has featured the same angular display units, but artists and designers have created unique artwork within each space.

For the redesign of the Instant store in Berlin-Mitte, Swatch approached three design practices located in three different cities. fuenteYfuente (FYF) is based in Zurich, Switzerland, and run by brothers Thilo and Alex Fuente. Pixelpunk (PXP) is run by graphic designer and artist Olivier Rossel, who is based in Biel-Bienne, Switzerland. Jacques et Brigitte is a graphic and illustration team based in Berlin, Germany.

The designers held several discussions via email, chat/messaging, and Skype, and met in Berlin one day prior to beginning work. They shopped for construction materials at the local hardware superstore, and returned to it daily during the installation process to purchase what they could not foresee the day before. They spent three days painting, building, and improvising, and the store was re-opened on the fourth day. Their installation blends paint, cardboard, and bare fluorescent tubes in an overhead assembly of colourful shards that challenges our perception of plane and dimension.

\01, 02, 07, 08: Suspended shards of cardboard were hand-painted in a way that makes them appear folded. Paint was applied to the walls, columns and ceiling in shapes that appear to have been projected from specific points.

\03, 04: The artwork challenges one's perception of plane and dimension. At times it dissolves corners, and at other times it represents three dimensions on a two-dimensional surface. Mounted at various angles, fluorescent tubes bring another level of dynamism.

\05: An angular aesthetic suited both the existing Swatch Instant display units and the complex architecture of the store.

\06: The array of angular display units is well complemented by the fragmented realm above.

FANTASTICAL

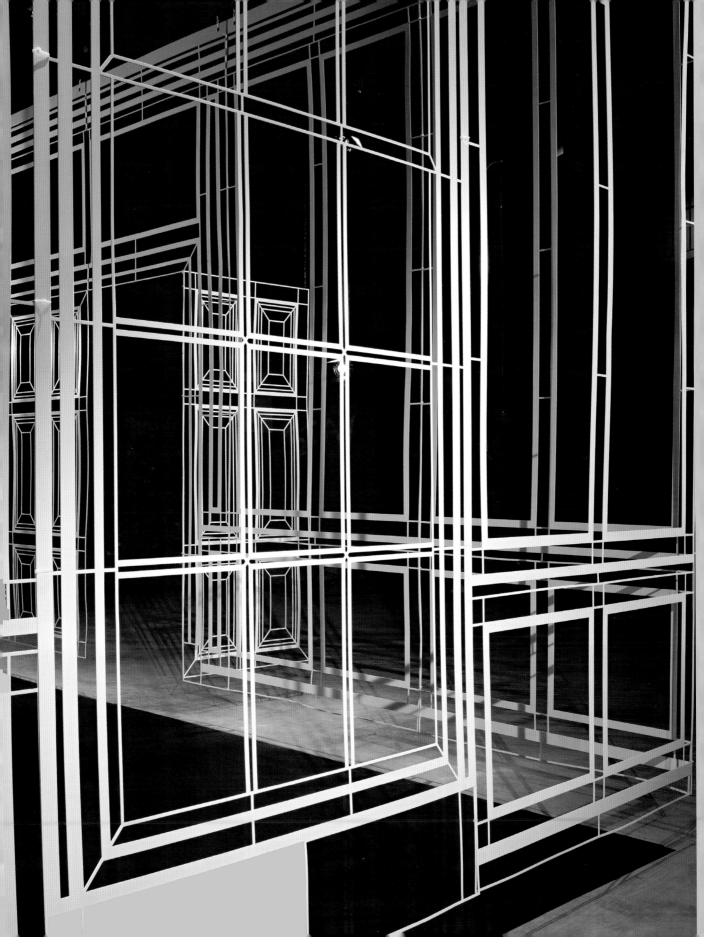

MONKI
3
SEA
OF
SCALLOPS

OSLO, NORWAY
design ELECTRIC DREAMS
photos FREDRIK SWEGER

\\\ An underwater fantasy world submerges
customers at Oslo's latest Monki fashion outlet. Both
beauty and mystery are offered in this dreamlike
realm, along with hints of imaginary danger. The
store was designed to offer an affective experience
of exploration and aptly reinforces the brand's
encouragement of creative personal expression.

There's always a new story to be told in the Monki world. This European women's fashion brand places as much emphasis on its store concepts as it does on its clothing, which combines Tokyo street style with crisp Scandinavian lines. The Monki brand promotes a lifestyle in which personality and independence are expressed, and dreams and imagination are encouraged. Monki's stores combine graphics, fashion items, and interior design to communicate an overall story.

The story within the latest Oslo store, at Karl Johans Gate 15, is one of a tantalising underwater playground. Stockholm-based designers Electric Dreams choreographed a multi-layered realm of mysterious beauty – a secret ocean domain with hidden treasures and deceptive currents. In this fantasy world, garments and shoes hang from sunken merry-go-rounds and tangled ropes in calm and turbulent conditions; bubbles of light float at the glistening water surface overhead; jellyfish tentacles shimmer; colourful water plants sprout; and the scaly skin of an unknown underwater being surrounds.

The way in which Electric Dreams have combined imagery that reflects both fun and danger is an apt expression of the thrill of exploration. By nature, journeys of discovery – be they personal or otherwise – require the feeling of being outside one's comfort zone. At Monki 3 Sea of Scallops, exploration of the store and the development and expression of one's personal style are journeys that overlap in a surreal and memorable manner.

\02

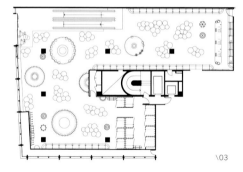

\03

\04

\05

\01, 05, 09, 11: Colourful sunken merry-go-rounds present an image that is both cheerful and deliberately ominous. The hanging garments and shoes appear to be affected by currents, hanging in regular and irregular formations.

\02: Strange flowers greet customers at the store's entrance. Escalators lead to the upstairs store space, whose ceiling can be seen shimmering from below.

\03: A floor plan (not to scale) indicates the staggered arrangement of the display furniture.

\04: Jellyfish tentacles drape from overhead. Dome-shaped light fittings are reflected by the ceiling and resemble bubbles at the water's surface.

\06: Low bloom-like display tables offer a field of merchandise on a mossy floor.

\07: Lacquered metal flowers house spotlights on the ceiling.

\08: Trumpets create a cheeky display rack for underwear.

\10, 12: The sales counter and perimeter walls bear unidentified white scales – apparently belonging to some unknown yet ever-present creature.

\13: In the fitting rooms, mirrors reflect one's image to infinity.

ULTRA

TORONTO, CANADA
design MUNGE LEUNG
rooster portraits STEPHEN GREEN-ARMYTAGE
custom lighting, screens, furniture, art DEVICE222, CASTOR,
APPLIED ART STUDIOS
photos COURTESY OF DEVICE222

\\\ In its previous incarnation, supper club ULTRA established itself as a place to be seen in downtown Toronto. After five successful years of operation, the owners felt it was time to push some boundaries. They welcomed into ULTRA a clique of over-scaled show roosters, and an extraordinary dose of peculiarity, humour, and intrigue.

The design of the eclectic supper club ULTRA gave designers Munge Leung the opportunity to revisit a previous project and dazzle ULTRA's customers once more. The designers introduced a clique of show roosters – over-scaled, preened, and proud – via immense photographic portraits by Stephen Green-Armytage. In doing so, they established a rich theme that ranges in character from graceful, to peculiar, to playfully humorous.

A number of Toronto creatives were commissioned to create custom finishes, furniture, and lighting in line with the theme. Thus, at ULTRA, one finds graceful, delicate feathers printed inside pendant lights designed by Device222 (who also designed the sheer photographic panels). Chicken-feather wall murals were created by Applied Art Studios. Inspired by birds, the cast aluminium legs of the communal dining table-cum-catwalk (designed by Castor) reinforce the bodily theme. Spindle-back chairs lacquered in cock's comb red provide a dynamic contrast to the butcher's block oak communal tabletop.

There is whimsy in such clashes, just as there is humour in the experience of dining beside gargantuan poultry. Cheekiness and playfulness abound at ULTRA, where, true to its name, an extraordinary and strikingly entertaining hospitality experience is to be had. And yes, chicken is on the menu.

\02

\03

\04

\06

\07

\01: Immense rooster portraits colonise the dining room, establishing a curious theme that is explored throughout the interior.

\02: At the entrance, Moroccan lanterns light the path to the main dining room.

\03: Pendants contain a flurry of printed chicken feathers, and red up-lighting dramatises a brick wall.

\04, 05: The sheer full-height portrait panels can be raised or lowered to shield the communal dining table for private events.

\06: Tall, sculptural candleholders were cast from deer antlers.

\07: The design of the communal dining table's cast aluminium legs was inspired by birds, and reinforces the bodily theme.

GREENHOUSE

NEW YORK, USA

design BLUARCH ARCHITECTURE + INTERIORS
photos ADO

\\\ Greenhouse is the USA's first certified eco-friendly nightclub. It satisfies various efficiency considerations, and was constructed with recycled and recyclable materials. To communicate its "green" DNA, it was designed as an expression of the richness of a living system. Installation pieces and matrixes of material create an aesthetic that speaks of the sciences while promising a glamorous evening.

Greenhouse is a nightclub, lounge, and event space in New York's Soho neighbourhood that aims to merge what are often two polar realms – spectacular nightlife on one hand, and ecological concerns on the other. It may seem an unlikely marriage, but Bluarch Architecture + Interiors crafted an aesthetic that speaks of environmental consideration while preserving the celebratory aspect of a night out.

The space conveys the dynamic richness of nature as a living system. Sustainable materials have been manipulated into an arrangement that suggests a gallery installation. A web of round panels, for example, appears to grow across the ceiling and walls. Some of the panels are covered with eco-friendly vinyl or artificial boxwood plants, and others house low-wattage LEDs. A total of 2,500 LEDs are connected to a custom-designed software system that allows for light effects in coordination with music or videos. The goal was to offer an experiential environment that feels alive.

Further contributing to this effect is the ceiling installation – a formation of 40-millimeter crystals that represent a shower of rain. Below, tempered glass boxes serve as tables, containing animal forms that rest on a carpet of eco-friendly artificial grass. Retrofitting existing systems to meet strict efficiency requirements was one of the architects' biggest challenges. Nevertheless, the savings in electrical consumption are estimated to be approximately 60%, and water savings of about 150,000 gallons (567,800 litres) per year have been achieved.

\01: Rather than a greenhouse, the large space feels more like a landscape.

\02, 03: An installation of crystals represents a shower of rain. The music causes them to vibrate slightly, and their appearance changes in the variable light created by lasers and LEDs.

\04: A matrix of round panels (or cells) creeps overhead. The cells are covered with eco-friendly vinyl or artificial boxwood, and others house low-wattage LEDs.

\05: Ceiling, wall, and table installations (such as matrixes and specimens) reveal the significance of scientific thinking in the design of the nightclub.

ANAN

WOLFSBURG, GERMANY
interior design HOSOYA SHAEFER ARCHITECTS
graphic concept BÜRO DESTRUCT
graphics FURI FURI COMPANY, FUYUKI, GWG, KEIKO
HIRASAWA, KENTARO "ANI" FUJIMOTO, MANIACKERS DESIGN,
POWER GRAPHIXX, YAMAFUJI-ZUAN
photos IWAN BAAN, UDO MEINEL

\\\ A slice of contemporary Tokyo resonates
unexpectedly within a German automobile
theme park. AnAn is a Japanese noodle bar that
contains artwork by a number of Japanese graphic
designers. Hosoya Schaefer Architects' angular
interior represents the chaos – as well as the calm –
of the Japanese metropolis.

AnAn is located within Autostadt – the German theme park and communications platform of the Volkswagen Group. The venue is well known for its contemporary architecture and its 60-metre-tall glass car silos, in which new Volkswagens are stored. Autostadt GmbH held a competition for the design of a small Japanese noodle bar, which would represent a piece of contemporary Tokyo. Hosoya Schaefer Architects' winning entry promised a venue that would hold its own amongst the impressive Autostadt structures. AnAn would be a heterogeneous space with an urban sensibility.

Customers are enveloped by a geometric framework of distorted hexagonal cells. These hover overhead on the ceiling as light strips, and extend underfoot as thin lines of aluminium in the polyurethane-coated floor. Some of the cells have been developed three-dimensionally with acrylic panels, and can be inhabited in different manners. They contain, for example, a counter, tables and bench seats, a coatroom, or vending machines, and are covered with artwork by young Japanese graphic designers.

These pods offer varying degrees of physical and visual enclosure, and create a feeling of spatial complexity. To develop the geometric framework, an algorithm was used in three-dimensional modelling software to minimise the number of angles and radii for the various panels. As a result, only two angles were used in the entire project, and the range of formwork required to construct the panels was optimised.

\03

\04

\05

\01: Artwork by various young Japanese graphic designers covers the 25-millimetre-thick acrylic panels that demarcate different pods.

\02: The acrylic panels span 3.5 metres from the polyurethane-coated floor to the ceiling.

\03: Distorted hexagons comprise the geometric framework. The space is illuminated by ceiling light strips that adhere to the framework of cells.

\04: The heterogeneity of Tokyo resonates via the varying degrees of enclosure and the sense of ordered disorder within the restaurant.

\05: Feelings of spatial complexity and delicacy reign within AnAn despite the over-riding geometric framework.

PEACOCK
DINNER
CLUB

GOTHENBURG, SWEDEN
design OLSSONLYCKEFORS ARCHITECTS
photos JAMES SILVERMAN

\\\ **Peacock Dinner Club – a glamorous and dramatic homage to its namesake – changes its colour and its function as the night grows deeper. As patrons move from the dinner table to the dance floor of this captivating Swedish venue, a dazzling light display subtly changes the character of the space.**

The chameleonic Peacock Dinner Club is situated two storeys below street level in central Göteborg, yet its display of light and colour rivals the most seductive of sunsets. This restaurant, bar, and nightclub drew its name and its theme from the long-standing Blue Peacock nightspot established in the same space during the 1960s. Wishing to pay homage to the venue's heritage, the new owners asked OlssonLyckefors Architects to infuse the venue with the beauty of a peacock's fanning tail.

The shapes, colours, details, and delicate shimmering quality of the tail influenced all of the architects' decisions. Dark, horseshoe-shaped banquette seats radiate around a white and gold ellipse-shaped bar with a circular DJ booth at its centre. Concealed lighting gives the bar a subtle glow, lending solid edges a feathered appearance. Light reflected off the gold-laminated bar counter creates a halo effect on the ceiling. A delicate and intricate golden panel handmade with 14,000 sequins creates a stunning backdrop to the bar.

Even more mesmerising is the seductive and iconic light show at the perimeter of the space. Screens of MDF, perforated with a peacock tail composition by graphic designer Nicklas Hultman, are backlit by a lighting system that changes in colour throughout the evening, from reds and yellows to blues and greens. As the restaurant transforms into an upbeat nightclub, the speed of the colour changes increases, adding another dimension to one's experience of this unique venue.

\01: Lighting plays a key role in this multi-functional space. MDF perimeter walls, perforated with a peacock tail design, diffuse changing multi-coloured light into the space.

\02: In the early part of the evening, black semi-transparent curtains bring a degree of privacy to diners sitting in the black leather booths.

\03: Dark-stained MDF ceiling ellipses echo the fan of the booths beneath, and reflect the golden light that emanates from the bar.

\04: Gold laminate, leather, colour-graduated carpet, and sheer curtains play with the rich lighting that seeps through the perforated perimeter walls.

\05: The white acoustic ceiling and white resin floor define the area between the booths and the bar, and absorb and reflect the coloured light.

NY 11-18-02-10

NEW YORK, USA
design CAMPAIGN
photos FRANK OUDEMAN

\\\ A grand Georgian house was recreated using little
more than aluminium during New York Fashion
Week in 2010. Bourdon House, the London home
and retail emporium of luxury men's brand dunhill,
appeared within a disused warehouse in New York's
Meatpacking District. It temporarily presented a
London experience along with dunhill's autumn/
winter collection.

Bourdon House was once the London residence of the Duke of Westminster. Now this historic brick property caters to gentlemen who prescribe to the luxury Alfred Dunhill lifestyle. It offers clothing and product retail, custom tailoring services, spa treatment, barber services, and a private screening room. The exclusive and finely curated experience reflects the heritage of the dunhill brand.

For New York Fashion Week, London-based designers Campaign transposed elements of this experience to the USA with an ethereal installation echoing the façade of Bourdon House. Twenty-two panels of white powder coated, laser-cut aluminium (just two millimetres thick) were suspended from strut channels to hover over a black rubber floor. Key looks from the dunhill collection were displayed in picture frames, and runway footage was screened above a fireplace. The sense of theatricality was heightened through the use of bright photographic lights, the arrangement of which was designed in collaboration with New York photographer Frank Oudeman.

The sense of a streetscape was created with vinyl wallcovering printed (at life size) with the exterior of Bourdon House and its Mayfair environs. The installation was accompanied by a modern interpretation of an English garden. Sights and sounds from Mayfair were projected for the enjoyment of visitors who sat on park benches that bore engraved plaques reading, "Alfred Dunhill – 1872–1959 – he would have loved this place."

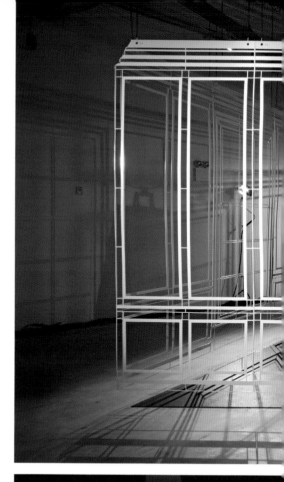

\03

\02

\04

\05

\06

\07

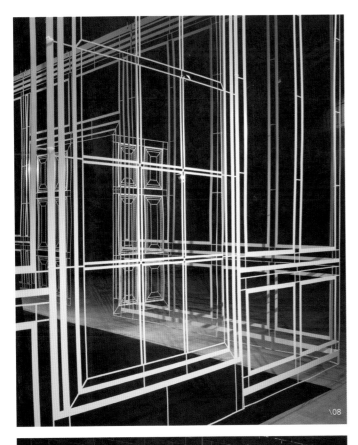

\08

\09

\01, 09: The Mayfair streetscape around Bourdon House was replicated at life size with printed vinyl.

\02: The panels of laser-cut aluminium composing the façade were each 3 x 1.5m in size. They hovered dramatically over the black rubber floor.

\03, 04, 05: NY 11·18·02·10 took up residence at West 13th Street in one of the last remaining archetypal disused warehouse spaces in the Meatpacking District. The various areas of the installation occupied a total of 600sqm.

\06: Each look was showcased on a custom-made frame and easel.

\07: Photographic lighting added to the black-and-white drama by casting layers of shadow.

\08: Georgian architectural details were reinterpreted in wafer-thin aluminium.

DANBO
FUN

SHANGHAI, CHINA
design MOHEN DESIGN INTERNATIONAL
photos MAODER CHOU

\\\ Danbo fun means "omelette" (with rice) in Mandarin – a food common in both the east and the west. At Shanghai's Danbo Fun restaurant, optical art effects, sculpture, and curvaceous furniture are boldly mixed. The aim of the design was to engage shoppers who view the space from above, and communicate the chaotic energy involved in making an omelette.

Danbo Fun is located in the basement atrium of a large department store close to the Zhong Shan Park – a major city park in Shanghai. The department store itself is ten storeys high, and has two escalators providing access to all storeys at the sides. MoHen Design International decided to capitalise on the spectacular overhead views of the restaurant space by invoking the vitality that exists within eggs, and the fast, chaotic process of making an omelette.

Massive and powerful gestures were needed for such a large space and the designers adopted both a literal and an abstract approach. The floor plan was derived from the shape of a cracking egg, with the yolk and egg white splashing out. The main entrance is through a curved tunnel structure that resembles the shape of an egg. In the middle of the space is a dynamic free-form sculpture that calls to mind the process of beating an egg in order to make an omelette.

The vinyl flooring makes use of the effect of optical art, in which static shapes appear to be moving. A composition of apparently rotating circles was derived, which gives the entire floor plane the appearance of mixing and bubbling. Pieces of bulbous furniture seem to float in the space like small yolks.

\01: Grand gestures engage the view of department store customers who may look upon the restaurant from as many as ten storeys above it.

\02: The central sculpture is the focal point as one progresses through the entrance tunnel.

\03: Optical art effects are utilised on the vinyl floor, suggesting the high-energy process of making an omelette.

\04: The restaurant is contained by a cracked eggshell or a pan, depending on your view.

\05: The thickness of the low perimeter wall is expressed through slits.

\04

\05

VENUEZ
WONDERBAR

AMSTERDAM, THE NETHERLANDS

graphic design EELCO VAN DEN BERG
concept and production WINK
photos ERNST VAN DEURSEN

\\\ For a yearly hospitality and style event in Amsterdam, illustrator Eelco van den Berg and creative agency Wink created a mind-bending 1960s-inspired bar setting that was open for just two days. Specially designed wallpaper, flooring, and graphics incorporating optical art and pop art influences transported guests to a dynamic party environment.

Venuez is a yearly exhibition event for the Dutch hospitality industry. In 2008 it was held at the Amsterdam Convention Factory – a large black box space that can be adjusted to suit events of various sizes. Design, communication, and event agency Wink was commissioned for the conceptualisation and production of a bar there, and engaged illustrator Eelco van den Berg to visualise an environment that would fill its guests with a sense of wonder.

The Wonderbar was to offer the central experience of Venuez, and as such, it needed to be evocative and memorable. Wink wished to completely immerse guests in the Wonderbar world, and chose a high-impact design direction that could be appropriately applied across a variety of mediums. van den Berg embraced the pop art and op art theme, and devised designs for wallpapers, light boxes, projections, carpet, and more.

A long, curtained entrance corridor served to build anticipation while it transported guests into the main space. Underfoot was carpet that had been custom-printed with a perspective-bending optical effect. Overhead, light boxes bearing pop-style graphics built up an aura of theatricality. Staff in hooped dresses welcomed guests into the bar, where boldly printed carpet, comic-style wallpapers, mirrors, and entrancing image projections delivered a wondrous experience.

\01: Carpet in the long entrance corridor was custom-printed with an optical art-inspired design, and served to disengage visitors from the exhibition context.

\02: Boldly printed carpet, mirrors, and changing visual projections combined to immerse visitors in a wondrous environment.

\03: To increase the perception of immersion in the environment, the carpet was also applied to the front of the DJ's console and bar counter.

\04: Light boxes bearing pop art-style graphics established a fun, theatrical aura as guests approached the bar.

\05: The concept extended to the realms of performance and interaction. Staff in hooped dresses greeted and served guests.

\06: Graphics on wallpaper behind the bar were inspired by comics and pop art.

CRISTAL
BAR

HONG KONG, CHINA
art and design KATRIN OLINA
photos HARLIM DJAUHAR WINATA

\\\ An alternate world exists within Hong Kong's
Cristal Bar. Immersive graphic installations have
transformed the entire interior into a canvas. The
result is a transcendent confluence of image and
physical boundaries where fantasy and reality are
fused, and the night is what you make it.

On the ninth floor of a tower in central Hong Kong, Icelandic artist and designer Katrin Olina has created a visually rich, abstract world that calls for profoundly personal interpretations. At Cristal Bar, Olina's explorative graphic art has been applied as a consistent visual language across the entire interior. Covering the walls, the floor, and the ceiling, it demands the interaction of the viewer. It moves well beyond the role of a backdrop, instead calling upon the viewer to interpret the imagery with their own set of memories.

Within the art one might discern flora, fauna, and mixtures of both. The imagery is layered such that a three-dimensional quality is achieved on flat surfaces. The computer-generated graphic art was printed onto film in order to be applied at the scale it has been within Cristal Bar. Although the bar contains four interconnected areas, the interior has become one seamless painting.

Lighting effects augment the immersive effect, and sleek furniture – specially designed for the project by Michael Young – plays up the otherworldly theme with formal references to 1960s space age furniture. A galaxy of 300,000 crystals encrust the bar countertop, and a ripple projector illuminates them with waves of varying hues. It is yet another surface for contemplation in this transcendental space.

\02

\03

\01: The furniture was specially designed for Cristal Bar by Michael Young, and plays up the otherworldly theme with formal references to 1960s space age furniture.

\02: Flora, fauna, and fantastical mixtures of both can be detected in the multi-layered artwork.

\03: The artwork is printed on glossy film, which covers the floor, walls, and ceiling throughout the bar.

\04, 06: In the zones where separate spaces meet, the different colours in the artwork are blended, further distorting one's perception of dimension.

\05: The impressive bar counter is studded with 300,000 crystals.

\04

\05

\06

SNOG PURE FROZEN YOGURT

LONDON, UK

interior and lighting design CINIMOD STUDIO
photos COURTESY OF CINIMOD STUDIO

\\\ "Life's brighter when you Snog," claimed an advertising campaign for Britain's Snog Pure Frozen Yogurt. In the context of cold northern winters and temperate summers, cheekily named Snog takes a witty approach to the sale of frozen yogurt. Its fourth London outlet is a quirky and colourful space that evokes the feeling of a perpetual summer.

Snog Pure Frozen Yogurt aims to communicate a message of health, warmth, and positivity through the design of its outlets. Building upon the brand identity created by Ico Design, Cinimod Studio has created fresh, interactive interiors for Snog's small chain of outlets in London. The fourth of these is located in Covent Garden, and incorporates elements from previous stores (such as grass-print floors, floral graphics, and digital sky ceilings) while also speaking of its site.

The retail space on Garrick Street was once the location of an apple store that dated back to the 1860s. This inspired Cinimod Studio to develop a modern-day orchard. Further inspiration was drawn from the dream-like world of Alice in Wonderland, and as a result, two surreal twisting trees stretch toward an animated canopy of LED lights. The glossy, abstract tree forms stop playfully short of the canopy, which dips and peaks overhead.

This undulating light field is composed of low-wattage LEDs within frosted glass spheres. Each sphere fixture contains three tricolour LEDs and is capable of millions of colours. Like a bubbling summer sky, the LEDs change the colour and thus the mood of the store throughout the day and evening. The installation creates the impression of a perfect, never-ending summer and bestows a haven-like presence upon the store.

\06

\07

\08

\09

\10

\01: Applied to upstairs windows, Snog's signature vivid pink creates a recognisable beacon in Covent Garden.

\02: A fully glazed streetfront and a generous ceiling height lend maximum impact to the lighting installation.

\03, 04, 05: The rippling canopy of lights provides passersby and customers with a bold, changeable, and memorable display.

\06: To create the bubbling globe ceiling, Cinimod Studio designed its own light fixture and oversaw its manufacture. Each globe hangs on its own cable and contains an individually addressable LED.

\07: A signature vivid pink wall and a gleaming white counter present an impression of freshness.

\08, 10: Marcel Wanders' Shitake Stools complement an organically styled communal bench that is suggestive of a fallen tree branch. The seating places customers in the proximity of the grassy floor.

\09: Grass-print vinyl flooring contributes to the carefree, summery atmosphere.

\11: The fascia features an array of vertical slats of pink acrylic – another of Snog's signature elements.

\12, 13, 14: The surreal, twisting trees are a reference to the site's former life as an apple store. Vinyl cut-out artwork was applied to the gleaming white glass walls.

SOQS

NISHINOMIYA, JAPAN
design KEIKO + MANABU
photos TAKUMI OTA

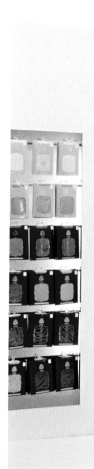

\\\ At the SOQS sock boutique in Nishinomiya, Japan, buying legwear is a curious adventure. The experience of searching for one's favourite book at the library inspired this surreal book-themed interior, where every page tells a story and the story continues from page to page.

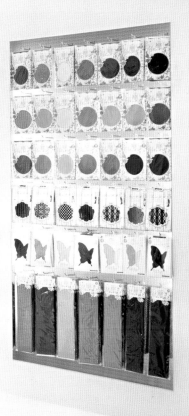
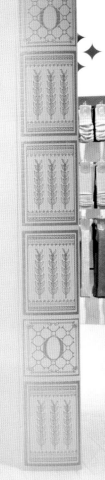

There is the implicit promise of a mental journey in any library. One's reading adventure is preceded by the perusal of shelves and shelves of books – a process that builds one's sense of anticipation. The library-goer's curiosity and expectation of discovery are piqued as they search for and locate their desired title and imagine the revelations that will follow.

Aiming to stir such fervour in shoppers, Japanese designers KEIKO + MANABU created an over-scaled book-scape for sock and legwear boutique SOQS. Imagining the store as a library of socks, the designers created the opportunity for customers to seek out their desired pair among book-shaped display racks. The humorous juxtaposition of themes was taken to the extreme through the styling of the display racks as formal hardcover books with decorative gold foil on their spines.

SOQS is located in a shopping mall – Hankyu Nishinomiya Gardens – and various measures were taken by the designers to draw customers into the store and to generate curiosity. The coloured book covers and white pages were staggered to create folding vertical planes that divide the floor area into zones and encourage exploration. Oval book trims were cut away to create openings and a layered view of the stock beyond. The interior was given a white shell and was evenly illuminated by uplights. These are concealed within niches at the top of each book. This lighting effect eliminates harsh shadows and encourages customers to circulate and experience an extraordinary environment.

\02

\03

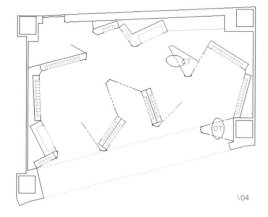

\04

\06

\01: A surreal and layered display system ignites curiosity and anticipation, and brings excitement to the purchase of socks and legwear.

\02: The unobstructed storefront maximises the visual impact of the book covers and entices customers to enter and explore the space.

\03: Large pieces of white vinyl flooring (sized 900 x 150mm) are arranged in a herringbone design that balances with the scale of the books.

\04: A floor plan (not to scale) shows the staggered arrangement of display racks and mirrors that lures customers through the store.

\05: Design elements developed from books include gold-mirror stars, oval-shaped openings, and a slight curvature of the book spines.

\06: Oval-shaped display benches protrude invitingly past the book covers and encourage examination of the featured items.

D'ESPRESSO

NEW YORK, USA
design NEMAWORKSHOP
photos DAVID JOSEPH

\\\ Cafés have always gone hand-in-hand with social interaction, serving as places to meet and talk as much as venues for the consumption of coffee. The sharing of perspectives over coffee and the consideration of alternate points of view take on a whole new meaning at D'Espresso, which represents a library turned on its side.

\01

Things are not what they seem at New York espresso bar D'Espresso. The venue is the first of what is hoped to be a chain of establishments and required a strong image for the emerging brand. New York-based interior design and architecture firm nemaworkshop was asked to develop a creative environment that connects to its location on Madison Avenue near Grand Central Station. The designers developed a bold concept that will be easily transferred to other locations.

Inspiration was drawn from the nearby Bryant Park Library. Hinting at the many perspectives offered by books, the designers devised an unusual but striking interior identity. At D'Espresso, customers walk on the bookshelves and recline against the floor. Pendant lights protrude sideways to cantilever overhead (rather than hang vertically), and books appear to be suspended above.

The bookshelf effect was achieved through the printing of full-size sepia-toned photographs on custom tiles. Stately deep brown timber boards were laid in a herringbone pattern on a side wall to represent a floor. The frosted glass wall behind the service counter represents a ceiling and illuminates the space. Small round white tables provide a visual balance to the sideways pendants, while transparent plastic chairs encourage the perception of floating above the shelves of books.

\03

\04

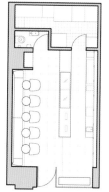

\02

\01: D'Espresso demands the unusual experience of walking on bookshelves.

\02: A plan (not to scale) shows the neat division of the space into serving space and table space.

\03: A narrow bar at the front window serves as an espresso-drinking counter and as illuminated signage.

\04: The chairs and banquette seat were designed to have minimal visual impact on the space.

\05: The white service counter aligns visually with the illuminated "ceiling."

DESIGNER \ ARTIST DIRECTORY

Ab Rogers Design
www.abrogers.com

Applied Art Studios
www.appliedartstudios.com

Artek
www.artek.fi

Asylum
www.theasylum.com.sg

Bernardo Bento (a.k.a. JEKILL)
www.jekill.net

Blocher Blocher Shops
www.blocherblocher.com

Blue Lemon
www.bluelemon.nl

Bluarch Architecture + Interiors
(Antonio Di Oronzo)
www.bluarch.com

Bobby Luo
www.thebutterfactory.com

Burneverything
www.burneverything.co.uk

Buj+Colón Arquitectos
www.buj-colon.com

Büro Destruct
www.burodestruct.net

BVD
www.bvd.se

Campaign
www.campaigndesign.co.uk

Castor
www.castordesign.ca

Chris Briffa Architects
www.chrisbriffa.com

Cinimod Studio
www.cinimodstudio.com

Claudio Reston (a.k.a. Haroldinho)
www.chacundum.com

Device222
www.device222.com

Dizel&Sate
www.dizelsate.com

DP Architects
www.dpa.com.sg

dw-squared (formerly Douglas Wallace
Architects and Designers), Hugh Wallace
www.dw-squared.com

eBoy
www.hello.eboy.com

Eelco van den Berg
www.eelcovandenberg.com

Electric Dreams
www.electricdreams.se

EXPOLAB Advanced Communication
and Design
www.expolab.de

Fefe Talavera
www.fefetalavera.blogspot.com

Felice Varini
www.varini.org

fFurious
www.ffurious.com

Formavision
www.formavision.info

fuenteYfuente
www.fyf.ch

Furi Furi Company
www.furifuri.com

Fuyuki
fuyuki.secret.jp

Garry Cohn
www.garrycohn.com

Giles Miller
www.gilesmiller.com

Gloss Creative
www.glosscreative.com.au

Glowacka Rennie Architects
www.glowacka-rennie.com

GWG
www.gwg.ne.jp

Guise
www.guise.se

Hawaii Design
www.hawaiidesign.co.uk

Hosoya Schaefer Architects
www.hosoyaschaefer.com

Ippolito Fleitz Group – Identity Architects
www.ifgroup.org

Jacques et Brigitte
www.jacquesetbrigitte.com

Jeremyville
www.jeremyville.com

Joey Ho Design
www.joeyhodesign.com

Jon Burgerman
www.jonburgerman.com

Katrin Olina
www.katrin-olina.com

KEIKO + MANABU
www.keikomanabu.com

Kentaro "Ani" Fujimoto
www.raredrop.jp

KINZO
www.kinzo-berlin.de

Koncept Stockholm
www.koncept.se

kwas (kensuke watanabe architecture studio)
www.kwas.jp

Make Creative
www.make.net.au

Maniackers Design
www.mks.jp.org

Ministry of Design
www.modonline.com

MoHen Design International
www.mohen-design.com

Momorobo
www.momorobo.com

Mr Important
www.misterimportant.com

Munge Leung
www.mungeleung.com

nemaworkshop
www.nemaworkshop.com

Nomad Ink (Tyler Johnson and
Flavia Sanches)
www.nomadink.com

Norbert Attard
www.norbertattard.com

OlssonLyckefors Architects
www.olssonlyckefors.se

Pablo Téllez
www.pablotellez.es

Peskimo
www.peskimo.com

:phunk studio
www.phunkstudio.com

Pixelpunk
www.pixelpunk.ch

Power Graphixx
www.power-graphixx.com

Projekttriangle Design Studio
www.projekttriangle.com

R2 Architecture
www.r2architecture.co.uk

RAISERLOPES architects//interior architects
www.raiserlopes.com

Rafael de Cárdenas (Architecture At Large)
www.architectureatlarge.com

Renato Faccini and Sunder Raj
www.estabelecimento.com.br

Rimon Guimarães
www.banzaistudio.com.br

Rinzen
www.rinzen.com

Salmon Design
www.salmondesign.com.au

Scott Weston Architecture & Design
www.swad.com.au

Stephen Green-Armytage
www.stephengreenarmytage.com

The Wilson Brothers
www.wilsonbrothers.co.uk

Tjep.
www.tjep.com

Tokidoki
www.tokidoki.it

Tristan Rault
www.tristanrault.com

UXUS
www.uxus.com

W1 Studio
www.w1-studio.co.uk

Wink
www.welcometowink.nl

x architekten
www.xarchitekten.at

Yamafuji-Zuan
www.yamafuji-zuan.net

Zaha Hadid Architects
www.zaha-hadid.com

ZMIK
www.zmik.ch

Zwei Interiors Architecture
www.zwei.com.au

acknowledgements

an\b editions expresses its gratitude to the many architects, designers, and artists who have contributed their exciting work to *Interior Pop!* as well as the photographers who have allowed us to feature their shots. We also extend our thanks to the occupants and owners of the featured interiors for allowing us to share them with our readers.

Interior Pop! is the second title to be produced by an\b editions. We look forward to creating many more.

\\\